I0465490

PRAISE FOR *THICK RED LINE*

"Having worked side by side at the FDIC following the 2007-2008 Global Economic Crisis, I have no doubt that Tory Haggerty's latest book *Thick Red Line* will provide greater awareness and real-world insights to industry experts, fair and responsible banking professionals, and other audiences as well. Lauded as a certified regulatory compliance manager and fair lending expert, Tory continues to raise the bar by adding value to the banking and consumer compliance community. This publication will be included in my personal library to reference as a regulatory compliance subject matter expert or leverage as an academic lecturer."

—VINCENT COE, JD, CRCM, Business Law Adjunct Professor

"Tory Haggerty hits the nail on the head regarding illegal discrimination in today's world '…most of the time, we don't even know it is happening. You must investigate the facts and data to find it.' *Thick Red Line* provides valuable fair lending insight from one of the best in the business and challenges you to be part of the solution. Get on board! '…through effective fair lending education and anti-racist policies, we can begin to solve those problems and prevent their reoccurrence. Let's get started.' I couldn't have said it better myself."

—JEROD MOYER, Director of Training,
Banker's Compliance Consulting

"By outlining the problems and following them up with solutions, Tory gives a blueprint on how to solve the historical issue of redlining. If you are interested in being an agent of change, this is worth the time to read and revisit in the future."

—MICHAEL MERRIWEATHER, JR, MBA,
Author and Real Estate Investor

"*Thick Red Line* by Tory Haggerty is a powerful call to action for social justice and an easy-to-read and informative guide that is a must for all fair lending compliance professionals. As someone who has known Tory Haggerty for several years, I can attest to his fearless advocacy and unwavering commitment to what he believes is right.

Tory's words resonate deeply in his book, particularly when he emphasizes, 'The color of someone's skin has nothing to do with the ability to repay a loan. I want loan decision-makers to look at the facts. Either someone is creditworthy, or they are not. Their race has nothing to do with it, and the law agrees. That is still not how it happens in actual practice, and that's what I hope to tackle in this book.'

This statement encapsulates the core message of *Thick Red Line* – challenging the systemic injustice of redlining and advocating for equity in all aspects of life. Tory's courage to confront uncomfortable truths and his relentless pursuit of positive change make him a true visionary and inspiration.

I wholeheartedly endorse *Thick Red Line* and applaud Tory Haggerty for his remarkable contributions to advancing social progress and fostering a more inclusive society. This book is a must-read for anyone passionate about creating a better future for future generations."

—**DANA GINSBURG**, Director, Customer Experience
and Communication, ComplianceTech

"Tory's first book, *Unfair Lending*, should be a mandatory read for all in the banking community. It provides valuable insight into the potential Fair Lending hazards in each phase of the loan lifecycle. In his follow-up book, *Thick Red Line*, Tory not only addresses the hazards to lenders but takes a hard look at the impact that redlining has had on generations of minorities. He provides valuable guidance on how to prevent, identify, and remediate redlining in addition to accelerating the service of minority communities."

—**JUSTIN SMITH**, SVP, Ncontracts

"In his first book, *Unfair Lending* Tory said he had a BHAG – a Big Hairy Audacious Goal – to eliminate illegal discrimination. Tory is the most driven and goal-oriented person I know so it's no surprise that after just two years, he's back with his second book to accomplish that BHAG. Tory has devoted his life to fair lending and this book provides more evidence of his experiences and research from which you can glean wisdom and grow as we work together to eradicate the unacceptable existence of illegal discrimination. Tory's BHAG is possible, but it will require all of us working together. If you want to be a part of this brilliant journey, *Thick Red Line* is a must read."

—DAVID DICKINSON, Banker's Compliance Consulting

"The regulatory focus on redlining has never been higher than it is right now. Tory Haggerty is a fair lending expert and his fair lending training and certification program helped me understand fair lending better even after decades in the business. This book is another valuable resource for bankers in the drive to eliminate unfair lending practices. While stemming from a very overt practice of drawing red lines on maps, today's redlining is much more nuanced and subtle, and Tory does a great job of breaking it down in easy-to-understand language and examples and showing how to end this practice. A must-read for today's bank compliance officer."

—JIM BEDSOLE, Chief Compliance & Risk Officer, BankSouth

"*Thick Red Line* provides excellent insight into the complexity of fair lending practices in the banking industry in today's market. Tory's expertise speaks volumes about the issues around redlining and corrective actions and explores concepts on how to solve and avoid these problems. At Encapture, solving these issues is at the core of our mission, and I admire the thought-provoking dialogue Tory is providing to the banking and lending community with his new book."

—TYLER BARRON, Chief Revenue Officer, Encapture

"I recently had the privilege of reading Tory's second book *Thick Red Line*, a deep dive into the practice of redlining and its impact on minority communities throughout the United States. His previous experience and compelling storytelling sheds light on the systemic injustices that have affected our nation for decades. Through his ability to humanize data, Tory's personal narratives and historical references clearly depict the consequences of redlining and repercussions financial institutions face from engaging in this practice. This is a must-read for anyone committed to confronting the injustices of the past and building a more inclusive future."

—JOSHUA KUMMER, VP, Fair and Responsible
Banking Manager, Bremer Bank

"Tory adeptly guides readers through the conflicted history and present realities of redlining, racially biased lending, and appraisal practices, offering real-world scenarios that shockingly persist today. It serves as an invaluable resource for anyone seeking to grasp these critical issues.

While we understand that instances of discrimination, although grim, represent only a fraction of the mindset within the banking industry, the examples are nonetheless glaring. This book serves as a vital tool in our collective journey toward equity and justice. By shedding light on the realities of redlining and racially biased practices, it compels us to continue pushing for meaningful change within the banking sector and society at large.

The insights within the book are not only enlightening, but also imperative for policymakers, bankers, and individuals alike as we confront the systemic racism deeply ingrained in our society. *Thick Red Line* is essential reading for those dedicated to comprehending and advancing equity and justice in our communities."

—NICHOLAS HARRIS, CRCM, Commissioned
Federal Bank Examiner

"Having been in the banking industry for 34 years I have had the opportunity to take many compliance courses; attend seminars and conferences; bank related compliance courses to name a few. Throughout my career I felt most of the courses I've taken would just skim over Fair Lending topics and I didn't feel like I really learned anything new. Several years ago I found Tory Haggerty of Tuscan Club University that offered a Fair Lending course. I was reluctant at first based on past experiences, but little did I know that his Fair Lending course was so different than any other course I'd taken.

The Fair Lending course provided by Tory and Tuscan Club University is by far the best course out there. Period! The course covers 15 different areas of compliance and also provides more detail and tools than any other courses out there. You can definitely use the tools provided within his course to build and even improve your Fair Lending program.

Tory also has a book that I read several times called *Unfair Lending – Why Discrimination in Banking Still Exists and How To Prevent It* which is a great book. Tory is very knowledgeable within the Fair Lending scope and has devoted his time and energy to not only help bankers improve their Fair Lending knowledge, but also help prevent discrimination."

—JEFF PETERS, Fair and Responsible Banking
Compliance Officer, Zions Bancorporation

"Bringing a passion that encapsulates his field of expertise, Tory brings the viewpoint of both regulatory and personal understanding about fair lending to every word he speaks and writes. Whether he is teaching his intense Fair Lending course through Tuscan Club University or as you read his books, *Unfair Lending* and *Thick Red Line*, he uses relatable examples to spur people to understand the injustices that occur due to discrimination."

—RALPH CARTER, Director of CDFI,
BankFirst Financial Services

"As a Managing Director of ComplianceTech, a leading fair lending software company, I am writing to wholeheartedly endorse Tory Haggerty's upcoming book, *Thick Red Line*, and to encourage you to add it to your reading list as soon as it becomes available. Having had the privilege of knowing Tory for several years, I can attest to his deep commitment to fair lending practices and his invaluable expertise in regulatory compliance.

Tory has demonstrated an unwavering dedication to promoting equality and eliminating racial and gender discrimination in lending. Through the Tuscan Club Consulting, his fair lending/CRA compliance training company, Tory has played a pivotal role in delivering high-quality compliance knowledge to our industry.

In a recent conversation with Tory, I was struck by his passion for addressing issues of discrimination in lending. His extensive background in regulatory compliance at the federal level makes him an authority whose insights you cannot afford to miss.

Thick Red Line promises to be an essential resource for anyone involved in ensuring fair lending practices within the banking industry. Tory's book delves into critical topics that are of utmost importance to us all. His frank and insightful exploration of redlining promises to deepen lenders understanding of fair lending issues and provide practical guidance for addressing them effectively. By reading Tory's book, you will not only enhance your own expertise, but also contribute to the advancement of fair and equitable lending practices across the industry.

I urge you to seize the opportunity to learn from Tory's wealth of knowledge and experience. *Thick Red Line* is sure to be a seminal work in the field of regulatory compliance, and I have no doubt that it will greatly benefit all who take the time to engage with its contents."

—MICHAEL TALIEFERO, Managing Director, ComplianceTech

"Tory's second book, *Thick Red Line*, weaves his personal experiences as an industry expert through the complex topic of redlining in America. The book provides a detailed overview of the history of redlining within the United States, breaks down recent case studies, and discusses the impact of redlining in easy-to-read language that is both eye-opening and compelling. A must-read for the financial industry and anyone else wanting to gain insight into redlining's impact on today's racial wealth disparities. As Tory states in his book, 'You don't have to experience something to care about it. Reading is a superpower.' I couldn't agree more. Highly recommended!"

—JOCALI NAKAO, Financial Institutions
Consulting Manager, Moss Adams

"Tory draws upon 15 years of experience in compliance and fair lending education to deliver a compelling exploration of redlining. In this book, Tory navigates the history of redlining, its persistence in today's financial landscape, and actionable insights into how to tackle the problem. Whether you're an industry professional or a curious outsider, Tory's straightforward solutions offer a roadmap for financial institutions to address this issue head-on. Building upon the foundation laid in his previous book, *Unfair Lending*, it is evident that Tory is committed to promoting fair and equitable access to credit. This book is not just a testament to his expertise, but also to his dedication to social justice and financial empowerment for all."

—DR. RAYMOND LEACH, Director of
Fintech, Augustana University

"I have known Tory personally and professionally for many years. He and I worked together as bank regulators and continue to stay in touch. This book provides an opportunity for the reader to capitalize on Tory's knowledge and experience in the banking industry, more specifically Fair Lending. The book defines Redlining in a regulatory sense and provides a more 'hands on' definition. It offers real life examples to help you analyze fair lending practices at your institution. It is a quick read that can help any person in your organization understand the issue."

—RANDY ROCK, Retired Federal Regulator

"In *Thick Red Line*, Tory Haggerty delves into the complex issue of redlining with precision and passion. Tory's dedication to raising awareness and promoting action is evident on every page, making this an essential resource for banking professionals striving for equitable access to capital and opportunity. For us committed to ensuring access to capital and fostering a more just financial system, this book serves as a guiding light, offering practical strategies and perspectives to navigate the complexities of fair lending practices and drive positive change within our industry."

—LINDA EZUKA, Founder and CEO, CRA
    Today and the CRA Hub

"Tory is one of the nation's thought leaders on fair lending, and in his latest book, he delves into the systemic problems that have led to decades of redlining in the nation. He tackles ever-evolving discriminatory practices affecting communities in our nation that continue to roadblock economic inclusion for all Americans. If you're a fair lending professional, this is a must read!"

—BRIAN WATERS, President, COO, and
    Co-Founder of findCRA

"Through industry experience and an understanding of redlining and its effects, Haggerty provides another resource for banking compliance personnel to educate themselves on fair lending laws, regulations, and common practices. Haggerty intertwines anti-discriminatory concepts with real-life examples to help the reader understand the necessary actions needed to forge a path towards a stronger and more inclusive economy. This book is a must read for fair lending compliance personnel."

—KEENAN NEAL, Knealson Advisory Group

"Tory Haggerty did an outstanding job educating people on the negative effects of Redlining. I love how he shared his life experiences and what led him to write this book. As a former regulator, I found this book to be educating, and eye opening. The recommendations he provides are spot on. Whether you are new to the banking industry, a regulator, social activist or policy maker, this book will help provide history and guidance about redlining."

—STEVEN DURANT, Retired Federal Regulator

THICK
RED
LINE

THICK
RED
LINE

WHY ENDING REDLINING CAN FIGHT
GENERATIONAL POVERTY AND
STRENGTHEN AMERICAN COMMUNITIES

TORY HAGGERTY

TUSCAN CLUB
—— PUBLISHING ——

Copyright © 2024 by Tory Haggerty

Published by Tuscan Club Publishing, a division of Tuscan Club Consulting
PO Box 91815
Sioux Falls, SD 57109

Printed in the United States of America.

All rights reserved. No part of this book may be reproduced or transmitted in any form or by any means, electronic or mechanical, including photocopying, recording or by any information storage and retrieval system, without permission in writing from the copyright owner. For information on distribution rights, royalties, derivative works or licensing opportunities on behalf of this content or work, please contact the publisher at the address above.

Cover and interior design: Heidi Caperton

Cover image of map © Hairem / Adobe Stock

Although the author and publisher have made every effort to ensure that the information and advice in this book were correct and accurate at press time, the author and publisher do not assume and hereby disclaim any liability to any party for any loss, damage, or disruption caused from acting upon the information in this book or by errors or omissions, whether such errors or omissions result from negligence, accident, or any other cause.

I dedicate this book to my wife, Erica. None of this would have been possible without your belief in me and unwavering support of my passions. I can never thank you enough for trusting me and letting me follow my goals, no matter how big or out-of-reach they may seem.

TABLE OF CONTENTS

CHAPTER ONE

WHY ARE
WE HERE?

If you purchased this book or received it from me personally at a conference, thank you for reading it. Discrimination in banking is a significant problem, and this book is another step in trying to solve it. If you have dedicated just a few hours to reading this, you have committed to being part of that solution by becoming more educated on the problem. Thank you for that.

Before we get into the topic, I want to tell you more about me, where I come from, and why I am so passionate about fair lending practices. First of all, this is not my first book on fair lending. In 2022, I wrote *Unfair Lending: Why Discrimination in Banking Still Exists and How to Prevent It.* The goal was to educate the banking community on why discrimination still exists in the banking industry. Don't worry. It's not a prequel to this book. There are no character setups or anything you need to know to follow along here. I recommend reading it, but you don't need to understand what is in that book to gain value from this one.

This book is self-published. That means I wrote it and put it out to the industry. I don't have a big company behind me, and I don't have what some people would call a "budget" to promote it. I wrote my last book and this book to share valuable information on an important topic because I want to make a difference in the few short years I'm on this planet. I've come to learn a great deal about banking and fair lending. I want to share the tools I've learned within the industry to make an impact in stopping (or at least slowing down) discrimination in my lifetime.

Since it is self-published and I'm relying on my skills, there will be mistakes in the book. Please overlook them. Instead, focus on the message. My goal here is to educate, not woo you with my knowledge and command of the English language (or lack thereof). So, who is Tory Haggerty, and why does he care so much about fair lending and discrimination in banking? I'm glad you asked, and I know just the guy to tell you.

Let's get a couple of things out of the way first. I'm an open book, if you will. (I promise I will only include a few bad puns throughout this book.) A few years prior to writing this book, my wife bought me one of those ancestry DNA kits for a holiday gift. I wanted to find my ancestral roots. "Maybe I have some DNA from some exotic place or something cool about my heritage...," I thought. Years ago, some of my dad's family members completed an extensive family tree where they traced back thirteen generations! They accomplished all of this in the 1980s by going through old courthouse records, if you can believe that.

My family's research even found that we were tied to a small royal family. I've yet to get a call from anyone saying they need me to step up to the throne and rule, and I'm not counting on that to fund my retirement, but it's a cool story. I also have about twenty male first cousins on that side of the family, so I'd have to "get rid" of many people I care about before I ascend to the throne. I don't see that happening.

Back to my story of the DNA test, I sent in my mouth swabs and waited long enough to forget I even took the dang thing. And then, I got the email that my results were back. Guess what I learned?

I'm white! White, white, and white! I'm whiter than sour cream, as Weird Al would say. Just quoting Weird Al Yankovic in this book tells you how white I am. If you don't know who Weird Al is, he wrote a parody song called "White and Nerdy" about how white someone is.

All of my ancestors are from the whitest parts of Northern Europe. My last name, Haggerty, is an Irish surname. We even have a Coat of Arms, which is also pretty cool. I also have a lot of Bohemian heritage, which I had to look up where that was. For all its glory, Queen's "Bohemian Rhapsody" lacks any geographical reference. Bohemians come from the Czech Republic. The point is, my skin tone, my ethnicity, and my race are all about as white as you can get. When it comes to discrimination based on race or ethnicity, I am in the least likely group of individuals to face discrimination.

If you look at the back cover of this book, you will see a picture of me. You will notice I have a beard. I've also used male pronouns referring to myself in this book. You've guessed it. I'm a male. I've been a white male my whole life. That's two for two in the "least likely to be discriminated against category."

As for my age? I'm not old yet (depending on who you ask), but I've hit the age where there are times I need to think about how old I am and sometimes even do math. I'm in my early forties at the time of writing this book. Now we're three for three. White, male, and middle-aged. Why would someone like me, who is the least likely ever to face discrimination, care so much about this topic? Let me answer that question the best I know how.

I once saw an internet meme with some of the best wisdom I've ever read. I wish I knew the author of it so I could attribute this to them, but I don't. I don't even remember the quote exactly, so bear with me. Essentially, the quote says you don't need something terrible to happen to you to care about the problem. That's quite profound thinking.

Something else you should know about me is that I am extremely curious. As a kid, I was one of those people who liked to rip things apart and put them back together to see how they worked. I always asked questions, challenged ideas, and wanted to learn everything about everything. The world is fascinating, and I want to see and experience it all. Too many people are born, live, and die in the same corner of the world without ever experiencing it. Not me. I want to do it all. With experience comes learning, and I love learning.

I also excel at pattern recognition and have an unusual memory for facts, numbers, and dates. I often see and connect ideas that others may not. When I see injustices in the world, they have a major impact on me. My mom told me a million times while growing up (literally a million because I counted) that "the world isn't fair." But why? Why, if we see unfairness in the world, can we not do something about it? It may be my nature not to shy away from a challenge, but I believe we can make a difference if we want to. We just need to put forth effort and try.

Too often, we don't care about an issue until it happens to us. That doesn't make us bad people; it just makes us human. We only have so much capacity to think and care about others. If it does not impact us directly, we are not likely to pay it much attention. I didn't care about cancer until my dad got it and passed away when I was ten years old. Now, I care very deeply about finding a cure. Does that mean I didn't care when others had cancer before it happened to my dad? No. It just means that when it happens to you personally, you see the adverse effects it can have up close, and you start to pay more attention.

I live in the upper Midwest, one of the most non-Hispanic white areas of the country. I didn't grow up in an urban area to see the effects of the topic I am writing about, but that doesn't mean I haven't studied it extensively. So many people who look like me don't see the issues and problems with discrimination, but I have kept my eyes open. I have witnessed discrimination over and over again, and I have to say that it is one of the worst and most powerful tools to keep an entire population of people down.

I like stories. I feel the human connection shines best through the power of storytelling. I want to share some personal stories with you so you can understand more about me and my motivation for writing this book and trying to end discrimination in the banking industry.

I grew up in a small town in South Dakota. Like the rest of the upper Midwest, South Dakota has a predominantly non-Hispanic white population. However, the small town I grew up in was on a Native American reservation. If you have never been to a reservation, they are unique places. The Native American residents are very proud people who value their heritage, but the communities are often impoverished with limited resources. Three South Dakota counties frequently make the list of the top ten poorest counties in the United States, and all three have reservations. The reservation I lived on was not one of those three counties, but it was not much more prosperous than they were.

For those of you unfamiliar with life on the reservation, owning land was a barrier for many years because of the sovereignty of tribal lands. However, the reservation I lived on, non-tribal members could own land. More than fifty percent of the community's residents were white, so Native Americans were technically the minority population, but not by much. There was also a community a few miles away near the tribal headquarters that was virtually all native residents.

A Native American school and community college were located nearby. In the town I lived in, housing built explicitly for Native

Americans was placed on the outside of town, away from the white residents. The housing for native families was often old and run down. Looking back, I now realize this was my first experience with redlining, even though I didn't know it at the time. In my tiny hometown of barely 2,000 people, we had redlining (which I'll get into detail later on and its impact on communities). For reference, we had to drive an hour to eat at McDonald's. We were a rural community.

My family lived on the reservation for decades before I was born, so I didn't know any difference growing up. Living on the reservation was just normal to me. I grew up among white and native children, and we all played together, went to school together, played on the baseball team, and had birthday parties like normal kids do. I didn't think much of race and why it mattered as a young kid, and that's the beauty of kids. They often don't see race or color as a negative trait. They must learn it. We could learn a lot by seeing the world through children's eyes.

As I entered high school, I noticed things my young mind hadn't seen before. Many native kids left the public school district for the native school, but a few remained and graduated as part of our class. As I got older and became interested in girls, I dated a few Native American girls. Around this time, I started noticing the racial differences. When I went to a party with mostly native teens, things felt different. The eyes stared, I heard the comments, and the tension was thick. The way some white and Native kids would talk to and treat each other in school troubled me.

I saw the differences in housing, income, and employment throughout the community. You didn't have to look far in my town to see the weight of discrimination Native Americans faced and how negatively it impacted their lives in nearly every way. Now, in my forties and looking back, many native kids I went to school with are gone, dead from suicide, drugs, alcohol, or just about anything else you can think of. Their kids are growing up in poverty without their parents, facing the same discrimination, and the cycle repeats. It breaks my heart.

If you are a person of color, you may read this story and think, "This guy is describing a random Tuesday in my life." If you are a white person, there's a chance you have never experienced something like this because, in the United States, white is the default. When you're white, everything is normal. It wasn't until recently they started making adhesive bandages in darker skin tones. Previously, every Black person who used a Band-Aid® had to use one made for a white person's skin tone, and of course, the bandage stood out. Johnson and Johnson invented the Band-Aid® in 1920, by the way. The point is that for many white Americans, you must go out of your way to be in situations where your race isn't the default.

After high school, I joined the active-duty Air Force. I left small-town South Dakota, and after basic training and technical school were over, I found myself stationed in Germany for two years. Every veteran knows the military is a mixing pot of people from all over the United States. I look back fondly on those times. My Air Force brothers and sisters took me in and treated me well. They also often made fun of me for being an ignorant, white, skinny kid from the middle of nowhere. I guess that, too, is part of the initiation of becoming a military veteran.

My Black service friends told me stories of how they grew up in poverty and with minimal resources. A different friend of mine recently shared that he always wears a collared dress shirt when he drives. He says he is significantly less likely to be pulled over and harassed by the police if he constantly wears business-like attire. I've been pulled over a handful of times, but never once did I feel in danger for my safety. It did not matter at all what I was wearing.

Fast forward a few years to when I was finishing business school. I started my banking career and headed down the path that led me to become a subject matter expert in fair lending. Banking has been and still is a male-dominated industry, but the part of banking I've specialized in is not. I had the opportunity to select my career path within banking, and I chose to specialize in regulatory compliance instead of risk management.

Regulatory compliance deals more with the laws, rules, and regulations that banks must follow. Risk management focuses on the strength of a bank and its likelihood of remaining profitable or failing. Fair lending is part of the regulatory compliance discipline. While general banking and risk management is male-dominated, regulatory compliance is female-dominated. If you ever go to a training session of compliance officers, a significant percentage of them are often women.

I also lead compliance group training sessions for different banking groups. I frequently travel around the country and train thirty or forty compliance professionals at a time. I am usually one of a handful of men in the room. It's fantastic that so many women work in banking. I would like to see more women in banking leadership roles as well, and we are getting there, but it's taking a long time. I've examined, audited, and consulted with hundreds of banks in over a decade and a half, and maybe two had a female president.

Since I've worked my whole banking career in compliance, I've worked alongside many great women. As a compliance professional in my different roles, I've been part of over 450 audit and review projects. That's a lot of different people I've had a chance to work for and with over the years. I've seen a lot of gender discrimination in the banking industry. It's not just men discriminating against women, which is by far the most common, but also women

9

discriminating against men. Since the compliance world in banking is female-dominated, gender discrimination happens in that arena, too.

I already mentioned that I am inquisitive, and I wonder why people treat each other this way. While I can't simply answer that question, I can try to learn and understand it. The human experience is so complex, and I am not an expert in that by any means, but I try to learn. When I started my consulting business in 2017, I knew I needed to get smarter. I committed to reading fifty books that year and hit my goal!

I read books on being a better leader, husband, father, business owner, communicator, and anything else that could help me. I also read a lot of books on human issues like discrimination. It's amazing what you can learn if you want to, and you don't have to experience something to care about it. Reading is a superpower. You get to download decades' worth of the author's experience in a matter of hours. It's a shame too few people take advantage of books, but you are right now.

While I grew up in a poor, impoverished community without a dad, things turned out okay for me. I've learned (through reading and personal experience) that losing a parent at such a young age turns some people fiercely independent. Losing my dad so young taught me that anything can be taken away from me at a moment's notice, so work hard and don't take anything for granted.

My childhood was extremely hard, but my race and gender never had an impact on where I wanted to go or what I wanted to do. However, race puts up roadblocks for minority individuals in nearly every facet of life. Major factors like employment, wages, and promotions are affected by race, and everyday activities as simple as driving without being harassed can be a daily struggle for people of color—something I take for granted.

I can't solve a lot of those problems, but I can try to understand the experience and empathize with people who face these problems every day. However, I don't feel like I am powerless. I can still make an impact. Over the last decade and a half, I have devoted my life to the banking industry, specifically fair lending. I've performed many fair lending audits and trained thousands of bankers to fix and prevent fair lending issues. That is where I can make a difference. The problems of discrimination in banking are solvable, and I want to share ideas on how to do that.

Let's wrap this up with one other form of discrimination I have seen all too much—the age component. I have already mentioned that I am currently in my early forties. Still, I saw age discrimination nearly daily in my younger banking days. I started my banking career as an FDIC bank examiner. If you are unfamiliar with that world, bank examiners are the federal government's suits determining a financial institution's strength or weakness. They are also the ones who decide if banks are following all the laws and regulations I mentioned earlier. Bank examinations are critical because the outcomes have multiple significant implications.

The numerical exam rating an institution receives can determine how much they pay for deposit insurance and how often they must suffer through examinations. In other words, it pays to do well and hurts to do poorly. Bankers are vested in performing well on examinations because much is on the line. For most organizations, an exam is just part of doing business. There is nothing secretive about it, nothing special, and they know what to expect because they devote resources to ensure they run a strong bank that follows the law. For other banks that push the envelope or withhold critical resources, many of which we will discuss later in this book, it can have a drastic negative impact.

As a young bank examiner, you have a lot of responsibility on your shoulders. You must "get it right." There is no room for error.

Many experienced examiners trained me, but as I progressed and earned my commission as an examiner, I was finally in charge. When you are a twenty-something examiner pleading your case against a bank president who has been banking longer than you have been alive, it is easy for them to play the age and experience card against you. This didn't happen all the time, but many experienced bankers did it and certainly did not try to hide it.

Now that I'm older and have a few years behind me and many more gray hairs, I can understand where these older and experienced bankers came from. However, if someone has a valid argument, attacking the person, their credentials, or what they think of the person's character will not make the argument invalid. For example, if I am a white American talking about discrimination—a topic I have very little personal experience with, but I have seen and studied extensively—and my arguments are valid and supported by evidence, then my race, ethnicity, sex, or age should not matter.

In the same way, if I am auditing your bank and have evidence that you are not following the law, trying to attack my experience does not make me wrong. Either I am right, or I am not. I often saw pushback from older bankers against younger examiners. Still, I found that if you keep your argument and facts at the center of those interactions, the age argument is ineffective. You can attack someone's lack of experience all you want, but that does not change the fact that you broke the law. While age and gender discrimination are common, race and ethnicity will be the focus of this book and how they play such a major role in the lending industry.

There is another reason I am passionately against discrimination and have devoted the rest of my professional career to seeing it end in the lending industry. The color of someone's skin has nothing to do with their ability to repay a loan. I want loan decision-makers to look at the facts. Either someone is creditworthy, or they are not. Their race has nothing to do with it, and the law agrees. That is still not how it happens in actual practice, and that's what I hope to tackle in this book.

Discrimination in banking is often not deliberate. Please don't misinterpret me. People can and do discriminate deliberately. I will give you examples of that. But what I've experienced and witnessed in banking is that most of the time, we don't even know it is happening. You must often investigate the facts and data to find it.

If you were to look at any random regional or nationwide bank, there would be no way for the average person to know if they were discriminating. You may suspect it, but that's far different than proving it. It is hard enough for highly trained auditors and examiners to figure it out. When a bank is accused of discrimination, the facts typically go to the Department of Justice (DOJ), and there is a long process to prove discrimination. It does not happen overnight.

While most banks do not set out to discriminate, it happens slowly and in little bite-sized chunks. As a bank grows, the problem spreads with the organization's growth until it becomes so large that it shows up in the data and becomes indisputable. It is my argument that racist policies and the lack of education on fair lending created much of the discrimination we see in banking today, specifically redlining. On the flip side, I believe that through effective fair lending education and anti-racist policies, we can begin to solve those problems and prevent their reoccurrence. Let's get started.

CHAPTER TWO

WHAT IS REDLINING?

The federal banking regulatory agencies define redlining as "a form of illegal disparate treatment in which an institution provides unequal access to credit, or unequal terms of credit, because of race, color, national origin, or other prohibited characteristic(s) of the residents of the area in which the credit seeker resides or will reside or in which the residential property to be mortgaged is located." What does that mean in everyday terms?

Redlining means a bank or other lending organization is not making loans in a particular geographical area, which is often a high-minority population area. I am going to use the term bank quite frequently throughout this book. However, banks are not the only institutions that make loans and can redline. When I use the term bank, it can also include a credit union, a company that does home loan lending like a mortgage lender, or it can be a non-bank lender. A non-bank lender is a small loan company that, like a mortgage company, does not take in deposits, but specializes in specific lending types other than home mortgages.

Redlining has been an issue in the United States for over a hundred years. Its history is simultaneously complicated, yet simple, because redlining is an easy concept to grasp. Banks do not make loans in minority neighborhoods. We can easily see and prove that with the right tools. It's complicated because so many players cause redlining, only so many resources are available to enforce the law, and education on the topic needs to be more prevalent. Let's look at history and see how we got to where we are today.

Most people associate redlining laws with the 1960s when the Civil Rights Act of 1964 and, later, the Fair Housing Act of 1968 made segregation in housing illegal. When most cases against lenders go to court, the Fair Housing Act is the cited legal standard. However, Richard Rothstein argues in his book, *The Color of Law: A Forgotten History of How Our Government Segregated America*[1] that redlining was made illegal long before the 1960s. The Thirteenth and Fourteenth Amendments made discrimination and housing segregation illegal 100 years earlier. However, the Supreme Court's interpretation and ruling on those amendments disagreed and thus put into place a precedent of nearly a century of forced and legal housing segregation that has affected every major metropolitan area in the United States.

If you have not read *The Color of Law: A Forgotten History of How Our Government Segregated America*, I highly recommend you do. It is the most comprehensive history of redlining that I have seen. Richard tells story after story about discriminatory policies and practices at virtually every level of government, from roughly the 1930s through the 1960s, that deeply segregated our metropolitan areas. When I say that deliberately racist policies helped shape the current world we live in, this is what I am referring to.

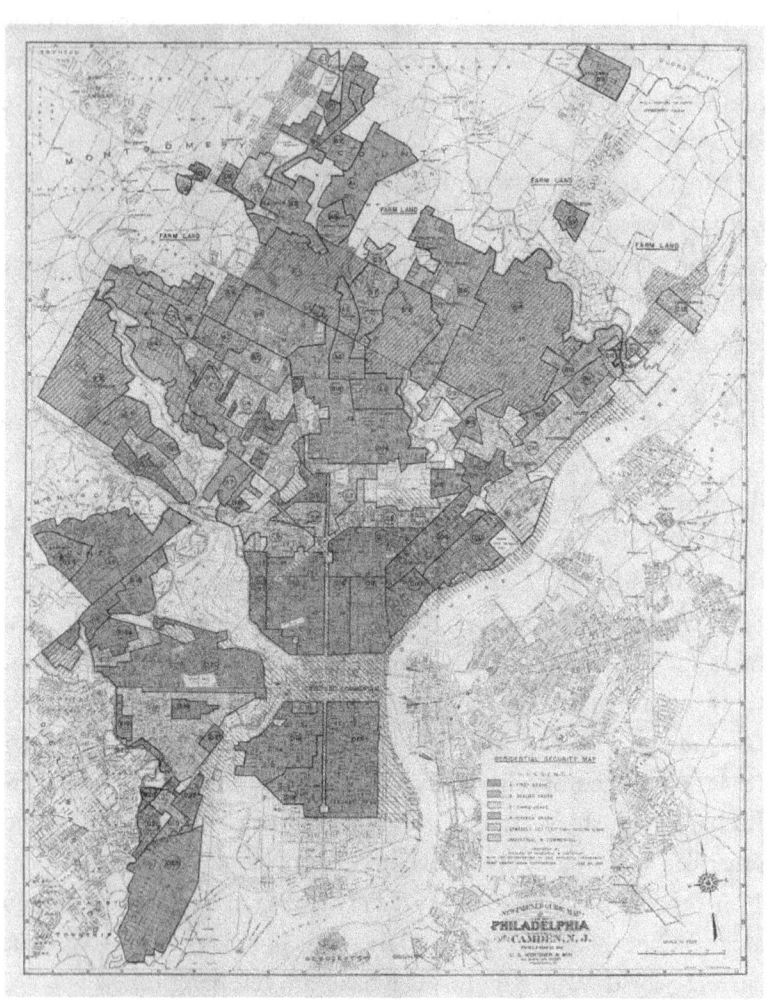

MAP OF PHILADELPHIA[2]

The Federal Housing Administration and later, the Veterans Administration would not guarantee mortgages for people of color or homes in neighborhoods where people of color lived. This sad fact ensured that only white residents could afford homes, and minority residents were forced to live in government housing and rent, often enduring long commutes to work. The communities designated for people of color were frequently located near industrial areas, power plants, or other undesirable areas like landfills. This led to a host of other problems like increased health issues. With little revenue from property taxes, basic community facilities and services significantly lagged in comparison to white neighborhoods or were virtually non-existent.

Suppose you read over that last part quickly. In that case, you may not have noticed I mentioned the Veterans Administration or "VA" played a significant role in redlining history. If you were an African American World War II veteran returning home after spending years of your life fighting for your country, you could not get a VA loan to buy a home that a white veteran could. As a retired twenty-year military veteran (Air Force and Air National Guard), this information grieves me, but it is part of our nation's history, and it is time to stop ignoring the truth.

The fact that people of color were denied homeownership for generations is a significant problem in our country. Homeownership is one of the most critical investments Americans can ever make. It is an excellent tool for building wealth, which can be passed down through generations to create generational wealth. You will hear me repeatedly share that fact throughout this book because it is worth repeating.

For decades, white Americans had reasonably priced homes and government-guaranteed mortgages at low interest rates, ensuring access to a powerful wealth-building tool. Minority borrowers were blocked from access, ensuring they could not build wealth for themselves or future generations like white families could. They were forced to remain in rental properties and government housing, as well as work lower-paid jobs with little chance for advancement.

The practices of denying homeownership based on race were not hidden. In fact, they were very much out in the open. Racial covenants were commonly written in property records. While this is widely documented, I want to offer a real-world example. In 2021, a member of the city council for a Kansas City suburb was doing research on chickens. She combed through courthouse records over two days to find out if homeowners in the area could legally have chickens in their backyard. What she ultimately discovered was a lot more alarming than just chickens.

There was a homeowner's association with a racially restrictive covenant that stated, "None of said land may be conveyed to, used, owned, or occupied by negroes as owners or tenants." There were 1,700 homes as part of the association, and it applied to all of them. These sorts of covenants can be found across America. While the Supreme Court made a ruling all the way back in 1948 that these covenants could no longer be enforceable, and the Fair Housing Act of 1968 also made them illegal, the wording often still exists. It is often a legal battle and costly process to have covenants changed, so while no longer enforceable, this ugly and racist part of our country's past remain.[3]

When you look at neighborhoods in America today, especially in major metropolitan areas, if you see high-minority populations, typically their neighborhoods are coupled with high poverty rates, higher crime rates, and low rates of homeownership. These factors have nothing to do with the character of these individuals. It has everything to do with the lack of opportunities given to them and their ancestors because of the color of their skin. Do you want another reason why I am so passionate about this topic? I believe that when all Americans can prosper in our country, our country will be better because of it.

So, the 1960s rolled around—the era of civil rights. The Fair Housing Act made discrimination in housing and, ultimately, redlining illegal. Problem solved, right? Not even close. Redlining was made illegal, but that did almost nothing to solve the problem. It may have prevented it from spreading overtly, but it fixed virtually nothing. Notice I said it stopped it from spreading overtly. It's still happening today, just not openly. It takes tools and trained individuals to spot it, but I can assure you redlining still occurs, and I will prove it through multiple case studies.

Think of it this way. You have generations of minority families with few opportunities in the workforce, poor educational opportunities for advancement, and very little wealth. They have lived in the same neighborhoods for generations, and now, they can "supposedly" move to any neighborhood they want. However, people don't magically pull up roots and move because they can. Even if they could, it is improbable they could afford it. The reasonable housing prices with low-interest rates and government-guaranteed mortgages enjoyed by white borrowers for decades after World War II were long gone by the 1960s.

Problems do not resolve themselves simply because the law changes. Deliberately racist policies created this problem, and intentionally anti-racist policies are required to solve them. You are going to hear me repeat that in this book, too. What does that mean? It means that removing barriers, like denying a loan because of someone's race, is not enough to close the homeownership and wealth gap. This point is what so many people need help understanding. They think the laws have changed, so everyone should be able to buy a home wherever they want, right? Somehow, we are now all on the same playing field. No. Many minority Americans were held so far behind the curve that just changing a law will never have a meaningful impact to help them catch up.

I'm not fond of politics, so I do not want to go too far down a rabbit hole here, but the solutions will be political. After all, we are talking about policy changes. I want to focus on all possible solutions, but we must recognize the past. This book is about education, and it is time everyone understood our entire history so we can build a brighter future. There are many books on racism and discrimination, and I have read and will likely reference several. Still, I want to keep the focus of this book on how to address the issue of redlining and general discrimination in the banking industry.

Redlining is still very prevalent in the twenty-first century. Many banks are still not providing equal access to credit, equal terms, or lending in higher minority areas at the same rates as in white areas. It is up to the federal government and bank regulators to identify these problems, but banks can help, too. Ironically, the same government that forced redlining upon our country (basically mandated it for decades in nearly every metro area) is now leading the charge to end it. I have not heard much for an admission of guilt to the problem, but at least we are moving in a direction to try and fix it.

If you have ever studied redlining, you may have heard the term "soft redlining". Soft redlining is hard to describe but think of it as a less obvious version of its elder sibling redlining. It's illegal, and very prevalent today. Until the Fair Housing Act's passing, redlining was allowed and forced upon our country. The laws in the 1960s made those practices illegal, but they still happen today. They are just not out in the open like they once were. In other words, the impact of redlining and the practices that lead to redlining are still happening, but they are much more difficult to see today, hence the term soft redlining. Redlining and soft redlining are virtually the same thing. They are both illegal, and every lending organization has at least some redlining risk that must be addressed.

CHAPTER THREE

CAN BANKS LEGALLY DISCRIMINATE?

I have taught bankers fair lending principles for over a decade. I spent a year writing and creating a fair lending school and certification program that teaches compliance officers and auditors in the banking industry everything they need to know about building and auditing a financial institution's fair lending program. I have had the privilege of teaching thousands of lenders basic fair lending principles.

I always start each training session with a quick quiz question. I included it in my first book and want to include it again here to illustrate a point. Take a moment to read and think about this question before you move on:

True or False: A bank can legally discriminate against a loan applicant.

Give it some time before you jump to conclusions. The question may sound tricky, but I can assure you this is not a trick question. Since COVID-19, I have had to do a ton of online training via webinars. While I have gotten pretty good at staring into a camera and at a computer screen while teaching and getting no feedback except for an occasional message in the chat, nothing beats being in front of a crowd. I love asking this question and seeing the looks on people's faces. Most people turn to their neighbor and say, "This guy's crazy," or "Of course, you can't." Usually, a few brave souls think outside the box and are willing to raise their hand and say it is true.

What is the answer? Can a bank legally discriminate against a loan applicant? Absolutely! They had better discriminate or will only be in business for a short time.

Considering someone's debt-to-income ratio or ability to afford loan payments is legal discrimination. It would have helped prevent a major housing crisis in the late 2000s. Calculating a loan-to-value ratio or using someone's credit history and score to determine their creditworthiness are also legal forms of discrimination. Those factors are called loan underwriting. Loan officers and underwriters use these factors daily to decide if they will make you a loan, how much money they will give you, what rate they will charge you, and the repayment terms. If you give money to everyone who walks in the door, you will make many bad loans, lose money, and likely will not be in business very long.

I know what you may be thinking—I tricked you! I didn't trick anyone. Those are legal forms of discrimination on who will or will not get a loan. That means that consumers should know how they are evaluated if they want the best possibility of being approved and receive best terms and rates. Is it wise to go into some big test or examination without studying? Well, lenders will test you to see if you are creditworthy. Why not know what the test is about and have the answers in advance?

You may have noticed I mentioned credit score as a legal form of discrimination. How we currently calculate credit scores has come under some scrutiny, and the way we calculate credit scores could change in the future. These changes may have happened if you read this book a few years after publication.

The problem with the current credit scoring model is how they calculate your score. Making timely debt payments has a significant impact on your credit score. Having monthly debt obligations and paying them on time every month is a key factor in determining your score. If you do that long enough, you earn a high credit score and are likely to get approved for a loan on good terms with the lowest rates.

What about people who do not use traditional bank loans? What about people who do not own their homes? Non-traditional payments, specifically rent payments, are typically not reported to the credit bureaus. That means if you are a minority individual and do not own a home (which we have already established many reasons why it is more common for minority individuals not to be homeowners), you likely rent. Those monthly rent payments are typically not reported to the credit bureau. Thus, your credit score is not improving to help you buy a home in the future.

You are living, working, and making monthly housing payments on time, just like a homeowner with a mortgage. Still, you do not get credit for any of those payments because you do not own your residence. Do you see how that is a problem? Suppose home lending policies have held minority individuals back from buying homes, and their on-time monthly rent payments do nothing to establish and build their credit history. How will they ever get approved for a mortgage in the future? It's a vicious cycle that keeps those at the bottom down.

The way credit bureaus calculate credit scores looks like a good candidate for a place to make a change. We don't need to get rid of credit scores altogether. The idea is sound, but we need to change the way they are calculated and the factors considered when determining a consumer's score.

The Fair Credit Reporting Act (FCRA) is one of the laws I have studied in-depth, and I frequently perform FCRA audits for my clients. The basic premise behind the FCRA is to establish a fair and consistent method for everyone to collect and report accurate information on a consumer's repayment and debt history. It's a good idea. Credit bureaus then take that information, create a model around the person's use of credit, and turn that into a number that becomes a credit score. They then sell that score to banks. That score is a major factor that helps determine the likelihood an applicant will repay a loan. With that information, it is quick and easy for a loan officer to look at a score and know that the higher the score, the more likely this person is to pay them back. But still, we must concede that the system is flawed and puts many at a disadvantage.

We discussed when banks can legally discriminate against a loan applicant using prudent and legal underwriting characteristics. When is discrimination illegal in the credit process? The simplest way to determine illegal discrimination is when a lender considers a prohibited basis characteristic in making a loan decision.

You may or may not be surprised to learn that no overarching regulation covers fair lending. No one be-all, tell-all, end-all law or regulation tells us everything we need to know on how to lend fairly to everyone. Many other topics in banking have one law or regulation you can turn to for guidance on doing it right, but fair lending does not. That is part of the reason fair lending is challenging. We need one place to go to find our answers. There are, however, several laws and regulations from which we borrow guidance, and somehow, bank managers and compliance professionals must put together a fair lending program free of discrimination.

The primary law cited most often related to fair lending is the Equal Credit Opportunity Act or ECOA. The ECOA says that a lender or lending organization cannot discriminate against a loan applicant in any part of the loan process on a prohibited basis

characteristic. ECOA gives us nine total prohibited basis characteristics that every lender and institution must follow:

- Race
- Color
- Religion
- Sex
- National Origin
- Age
- Marital Status
- Filing for protection under the Act
- Income from public assistance

This list means that you can discriminate against a loan applicant because of a low credit score or because their debt-to-income
ratio is too high, but you cannot discriminate against them because
of their race, age, sex, and other characteristics on the list.

The Fair Housing Act covers residential transactions, and that
law also has a list of prohibited basis characteristics. Lenders must
follow both the ECOA and Fair Housing Act lists for home loans.
The first five on the list are the same as the ECOA. They add on an
additional two that ECOA does not contain.

- Race
- Color
- Religion
- Sex
- National Origin
- Familial Status
- Handicap

These two laws and the list of prohibited basis characteristics give us the baseline for fair lending guidance in the United States. There is more to the laws, but that is the central concept. Most fair lending training for lenders lists the prohibited basis characteristics, gives the definition of discrimination, and cites a couple of examples of how other lenders have screwed up. How is that educational? How does that make a lender better at their job? How does it teach them to ensure they follow the laws and not discriminate? The answer is that it doesn't, which is a major problem. We lack sufficient basic fair lending education in our industry, which is one of the major breakdowns I am trying to change.

If you are in the banking industry, you may think I left out other laws and regulations. Other laws often get tied to fair lending, like the Community Reinvestment Act, the Home Mortgage Disclosure Act, or even the previously mentioned Fair Credit Reporting Act. I'm not ignoring these laws and their implementing regulations. I will be addressing them and their relevance throughout the book.

My fair lending education and training goes so much further beyond the basics. There are many chances to discriminate during the loan life cycle; every lender should know them. That's what we will talk about next.

CHAPTER FOUR

THE LOAN LIFE CYCLE OF FAIR LENDING RISKS

In my first book, I extensively discuss the loan life cycle of fair lending risks. The book focuses on these risks and what a bank can do to prevent them in much greater detail, so I will only cover them briefly in this chapter.

This graphic walks you through the process of getting a loan at a bank. Each step in the process holds fair lending risks every banker should know. Let's cover them briefly.

When you study the graphic, you may see that marketing is number seven. Marketing can also be the first step in the loan lifecycle process. I chose to put it near the end of the life cycle because marketers must understand all the risks to build more robust marketing programs. With that said, let's dig in.

LOAN LIFECYCLE

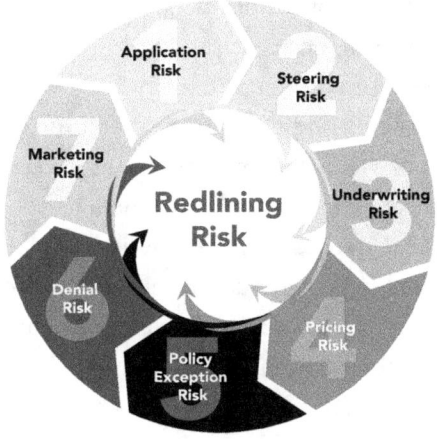

Application Risk – This is the first part of the loan life cycle. This step is where someone applies for a loan, and there are a few key ways an applicant can experience discrimination. An applicant may be straight-up discouraged from applying. During my career as a federal bank examiner, we had a complaint against a bank we were reviewing. A female minority applicant applied for a car loan with a white male lender. During the application conversation, the lender commented to the applicant, "I know how you people are with car loans." What do you think that applicant thought after hearing that comment? Spoiler alert—she was upset. She left the bank and filed a fair lending complaint. We investigated the situation as that was part of our job. This applicant was discouraged from even applying. Every applicant should be encouraged to go through the application process. The lender failed miserably in this case.

Steering Risk – Once you apply, lenders must figure out what loan product an applicant will get. They "steer" people into different loan products. This decision should result from a person's creditworthiness and need, but sometimes it does not. Minority applicants can be steered into higher-cost products even if they qualify for better alternatives. In addition, minority borrowers are frequently targeted for costly add-on products like credit life insurance, which drive up the cost of a loan. When an applicant is steered into the best product that meets their current needs, the lender has conducted a successful financial transaction. The law is likely broken when an applicant is guided into a product or service based on a prohibited basis characteristic instead of a lower-cost alternative.

We see this problem often with government-guaranteed mortgage loan programs. Yes—the same ones that minority borrowers could not access for decades are now used in illegal steering. Government-guaranteed loans can be a good thing. These loans get borrowers into loan products when they would otherwise not qualify. Still, they often carry hefty origination fees to help pay for the guarantee they offer. That means they are usually more expensive than traditional financing. When a minority borrower is steered into a higher-cost government-guaranteed loan, but qualifies for cheaper traditional funding, this may be illegal steering.

Underwriting Risk – Once you get the applicant into the right product, the banker must make the loan decision. This is a significant part of the loan life cycle because it determines whether someone will get a loan.

Remember, I mentioned there are legal forms of discrimination. You can deny someone because they cannot afford the loan payments. Suppose someone meets all credit standards, but they are denied because of race or ethnicity. In that case, it's likely a violation of the law.

Underwriting programs must be clear, concise, and free from discrimination. Giving a lender clear guidance on determining an applicant's repayment ability is a great way to build a robust fair lending program. Still, those programs often need to be improved within banks.

Pricing Risk – If a lender approves a loan, they must set terms and the interest rate. This step is essential because it will determine how much the loan will cost. The interest rate is the most significant part of the pricing step, but the repayment terms and fees are also crucial.

I have seen time and again where certain prohibited basis groups receive much higher average interest rates. My company performs dozens of fair lending audits annually, and we frequently see cases where minority or female applicants receive significantly higher average interest rates than white or male borrowers. Banks should be testing for this, but many don't.

Exception Risk – All banks must establish strong policies and procedures for making loan decisions and pricing loans. That is one of the backbones of an excellent fair lending program. Clear and concise guidance for lenders, free from guesswork, builds a solid, fair lending program. Following those legal forms of discrimination (policies and procedures) is the best way to ensure consistent lending decisions and reduce fair lending risk. However, lenders often request exceptions to the policy when an applicant does not quite fit in a box.

What if a loan product's minimum required credit score is 620, but an applicant's score is 615? They have plenty of money to repay the loan but had a bumpy past in making on-time payments. It happens to many people. Should that be a reason to deny them? They have been a bank customer for years and have always paid back loans on time. Isn't it reasonable to approve that loan request when they are barely outside of policy?

Some banks approve these policy exceptions all the time. Managers frequently approve loans outside of policy because banks need to make loans. That is how they make money. They take in deposits (money people don't readily need) and make loans (money others do readily need). That, in a nutshell, is how banking works. The more times a bank makes a loan, the more money they can make.

However, the more times a bank makes a policy exception, the more chances they have of making exceptions on a prohibited basis characteristic. For example, I've seen where a bank made exceptions nearly 95 percent of the time for men and only made exceptions for women 5 percent of the time. I've seen where banks rarely, if ever, make exceptions to minority borrowers but constantly make exceptions for white borrowers. That's where this practice becomes a fair lending issue and likely leads to discrimination.

Denial Risk – Denial risk is tied closely to underwriting risk. When a lender makes the underwriting decision and decides not to make the loan, it moves to the denial category. Data is one of the best ways to determine if a bank has a higher denial risk. Certain mortgage lenders are required to collect data on their home loan applicants. This data includes underwriting characteristics and whether a loan request was approved or denied. They also must collect the race, ethnicity, and sex of all applicants. So, reviewing that data can quickly show high denial rates for minority applicants. It can also show high denial rates in minority neighborhoods. This data is one of the ways banking regulators discover redlining.

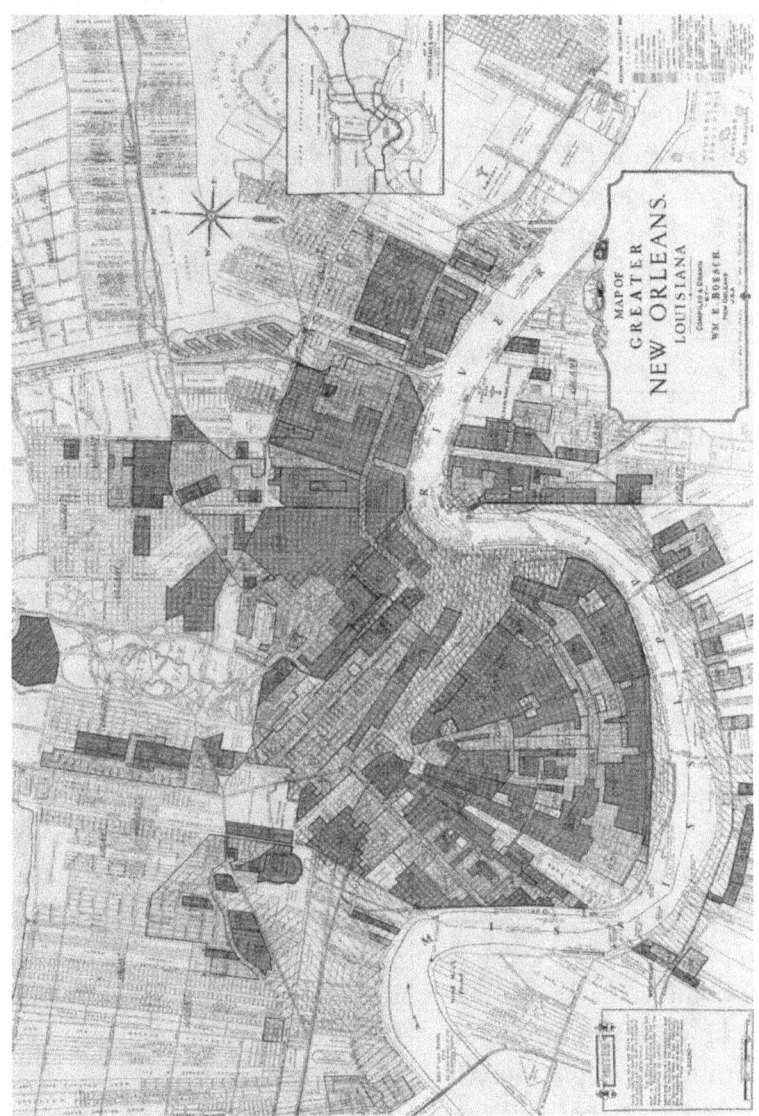

MAP OF NEW ORLEANS[4]

Marketing Risk – As mentioned earlier, we can put marketing at the beginning of the loan life cycle. Still, I placed it at the end of the cycle so we have a better understanding of what we are marketing and why.

Marketing risk dramatically increases when a bank targets specific individuals as customers. Most major fair lending cases cite marketing practices as a critical factor in discriminatory behavior. For example, if a bank only markets to white neighborhoods but not minority neighborhoods, where do you think most of their applicants will come from? If ads only feature white individuals and not minority individuals, what message does that send to potential customers?

Redlining Risk – I have already given a basic definition of redlining. This practice happens when a bank does not make loans in high-minority areas. Redlining risk is not part of the life cycle but inside the circle because all the other risks can lead to redlining.

In some instances, lenders screen applicants and discourage them from applying. Suppose an applicant shares a poor credit score with a lender during the application process. The lender may tell the applicant it is not worth applying as their likelihood of being approved is low.

Application risk can also cover the rate at which banks receive applications from minority borrowers and minority neighborhoods. Redlining cases often cite the number of applications from minority neighborhoods as a key leading indicator of redlining discrimination. That is just common sense when you think about it. How will you make loans in minority neighborhoods if you don't receive applications from those neighborhoods?

In the steering process, customers are steered into higher-cost loans based on their race, ethnicity, or where they live. Steering can significantly contribute to redlining risk if customers in high- minority neighborhoods are guided into less advantageous products based on a prohibited basis characteristic.

In underwriting, redlining happens when loan decisions are not made fairly and consistently because of where a customer lives. Suppose white and male borrowers are approved for loans disproportionately more often than minority and female borrowers, and they have similar creditworthiness. In that case, this can lead to a higher likelihood of redlining due to the segregated history of our cities.

For pricing, the same concept in underwriting exists. If specific borrowers always seem to get better rates and terms or pay lower fees, we can see this seep into redlining as banks do it based on the borrower's geography.

Residents living in minority neighborhoods sometimes pay more for loans on average. This risk plays out when exceptions are likely and prevalent in white neighborhoods, but rare in minority neighborhoods. We find this pattern in the data where minority neighborhoods see higher denial rates or higher average interest rates on approved loans. When finding out these factors and reviewing a bank's loan exception data, there is often a connection between the two. Exceptions are frequently made for white borrowers in white neighborhoods and rarely granted for minority borrowers in minority neighborhoods.

For denials, this again ties back to underwriting decisions. High denial rates in minority neighborhoods will lead to lower levels of lending, which is the core of redlining. I mentioned that application risk is critical because if a lender doesn't get applications from minority neighborhoods, it's tough to make loans there. Having high denial rates in minority neighborhoods also leads to low lending levels in communities of color.

Marketing risk leads to redlining when marketing efforts are put toward white neighborhoods but not minority neighborhoods.

Banks either devote significantly fewer resources or decide not to market in minority neighborhoods altogether. If customers don't know about a bank's products and services because they never market to them, this lack of awareness often leads to redlining.

As you can see, many factors contribute to redlining. Each financial institution is unique; however, there are common redlining themes and trends. In other words, most redlining cases have a handful of the same characteristics. They often share similarities that banks can use to help build a fair lending program free from discrimination. Data is still vital in identifying fair lending risk and redlining risk. However, one can look at an overall organization for certain factors and see a higher risk for redlining. I will cover those in the next chapter.

CHAPTER FIVE

WHAT MOST REDLINING CASES HAVE IN COMMON

There were redlining cases in the twentieth century, but they have become much more common in the twenty-first century. Specific laws like the Home Mortgage Disclosure Act (HMDA) have made data more readily available to aid in identifying these patterns.

Earlier, I mentioned that certain mortgage lenders are required to collect information on home loan applicants. In the banking industry, we call this HMDA data. Larger HMDA reporters must collect 110 pieces of data on every home loan application and report them to the federal government every March. The federal government then puts all that data together and releases it to the industry. You can review any HMDA-reporting institution's lending performance with the right software tools.

Lenders must ask every applicant their age, race, sex, marital status, and ethnicity. Some applicants choose not to report this data because they fear banks will use it to discriminate against them. The opposite is true. All applicants should always report this key data regardless of their race or ethnicity. The reason is that the federal government uses that data to determine whether or not banks discriminate. If applicants don't provide that key data, problems could linger much longer because the government or auditors like me will not be able to identify trends without knowing the demographics of the people applying for loans. We discover lending levels to different minority individuals through that data, so if an individual chooses not to report information, it hurts the cause.

Let's say you are a minority applicant and choose not to disclose your race or ethnicity. Suppose you should have been approved for a home loan because of your creditworthiness, but you are denied. In that case, the government will never know you were discriminated against if you did not report your race and ethnicity. That's why HMDA data is essential, why banks are required to collect it, and why everyone should offer it when applying. It is one of the key metrics used in fair lending examinations.

In 2018, HMDA saw its most significant change since its inception. Before 2018, banks only collected a few dozen pieces of data. In 2018, the law changed and significantly increased the available data. Where HMDA reporters used to collect thirty-nine data points on every home loan application, the new rules require 110 data points. With this new and expanded data, regulators can better see a bank's performance and if they are engaging in discriminatory lending practices and redlining.

Another critical factor that has increased the number of formally prosecuted redlining cases is the DOJ's Combatting Redlining Initiative, which rolled out in 2021. The government enacted this initiative to identify lenders engaging in redlining and hold them accountable—where redlining cases before the initiative were maybe one every other year, ten or more cases a year are now the new norm.

One of the advantages of a redlining case is that the facts and findings are public. The formal complaint and order against the institution are a matter of public record—all you need to do is Google it to find it. This insight means anyone paying attention can review how other banks have redlined and learn from those mistakes. You will see patterns emerging if you combine these findings, which we are about to do. Any bank can then look at its program, data, and bank structure to see if it, too, has a high risk for redlining based on what it learned in the settled public cases.

Sadly, many banks do not take the time to do this, so redlining cases continue. One of the goals of this book is to provide you with the data. I've done all the research for you. Investing in a fair lending audit is also expensive. Still, it is significantly cheaper than government fines, increased regulatory scrutiny, public enforcement actions, and the stain on a bank's reputation as a lender when their name hits the news for discrimination.

I've put together some common facts to educate banks on how to identify redlining risks. I have gained some of this information from reading public cases, and I have learned others from listening to regulators and DOJ officials at conferences and taking lots of notes.

FACTOR ONE – BRANCH STRUCTURE

The locations of a bank's physical offices are at the heart of most redlining cases. Time and again, redlining cases cite that a bank's branches concentrate in white neighborhoods and avoid high-minority areas.

One recently settled case was a bank operating in a major metropolitan area. As the bank grew, it opened nearly a dozen branches in majority-white census tracts but only one in a majority-minority census tract. A census tract is just a smaller subdivision of a county. The US Census Bureau uses them to help better show statistics of smaller geographic neighborhoods instead of an entire county. Just eight percent of this bank's branches were in high-minority areas. In comparison, more than 50 percent of the metropolitan area included high-minority census tracts. Deliberate or not, this bank was opening branches in white neighborhoods but not minority neighborhoods.

Branch locations are critical in redlining cases because they contribute to other issues. It's common sense that having a bank branch in an area is a key way to get applications from the residents in that area. Why would a loan applicant drive thirty to sixty minutes out of their way, passing by ten other banks, to apply at your nearest branch?

One easy way to spot branching issues is to plot branch locations on a map that shows minority populations. Many redlining cases show that a bank's branch locations make a horseshoe shape around the high-minority areas. This visual representation is a powerful tool. I recommend that all banks plot their branch locations on a minority population map to see if they find this horseshoe shape. It's the cornerstone of many redlining cases. Sometimes, numbers and percentages get lost in translation. Still, pictures of dots and colors are easily understood, and you don't need to be a compliance or fair lending expert to see the risk jump off the page.

FACTOR TWO – APPLICATIONS RECEIVED

I don't want to sound like Captain Obvious here, but this needs to be said. If a bank is not taking applications from minority areas, they will not make loans in minority areas. Like plotting branches on a map, a bank can use HMDA data to plot applications on a minority map to see the distribution of applications received.

Like with branches, this visual representation of applications is a powerful tool to spot redlining.

Another critical tool is comparing a bank's application and loan rate performance to peer lenders. Peer lenders are other lenders in a bank's operating area that also make home loans. They can be banks, credit unions, and mortgage companies that make a similar number of loans in the same geographical footprint. Suppose you look at a bank's application rates from minority borrowers and high-minority areas, and they lag in comparison to their peers. In that case, this is a crucial redlining indicator. When other lenders are taking way more applications than you, that is likely to happen.

One of the things the federal government does is compare a bank's performance to peers by a simple ratio. In other words, they will count the number of applications a bank received in minority areas and compare that to the rate at which peer lenders took applications in the same high-minority neighborhoods and express that as a ratio. In redlining cases, it is common to see peers take applications in high-minority neighborhoods two, three, and four times more often than the bank in question.

With the right software, a bank can quickly and easily see its performance and calculate the ratios. Regulators often cite lagging indicators like this as crucial facts in redlining cases. How will you make loans in high-minority areas when you have not received any applications? Here's another light bulb moment—banks not receiving applications often do not have branch locations in those areas.

FACTOR THREE – ADVERTISING AND MARKETING EFFORTS

The old saying still holds – "Location, Location, Location." To receive applications from a specific area, it helps to have a presence in that area. But marketing and digital banking are other ways to reach prospective customers. Today, you can start a banking relationship, open deposit accounts, and take out a loan without entering a bank branch. However, customers still need to know you exist to make this possible.

Redlining cases always look at a bank's marketing efforts. Did the bank focus resources in high-minority areas or deliberately avoid marketing their products and services in those areas?

During one fair lending examination I conducted, the head of marketing told me, "Our bank president said not to send home loan marketing materials to a certain zip code." I looked up that zip code, and guess what? It was a Native American reservation. They deliberately chose not to market in that area to avoid lending there, even though it was part of their trade area.

I have had conversations with other bankers who stopped marketing in high-minority areas because they felt it was not profitable. Their HMDA data showed that peers made loans three and four times more often than they did in that area. So, not only are their lending rates lagging significantly, but they have also stopped devoting resources to marketing and trying to bring in new applications. I wish I were making this up. I quickly recommended that this bank reinvest in marketing, but I'm afraid to say that recommendation fell on deaf ears. Their previous marketing efforts did not bring in new applications, so they quit as they were trying to save money. It's only a matter of time now before they become another statistic.

FACTOR FOUR – LOAN ORIGINATION RATES

This one shouldn't come as a shock, but the rate at which a bank originates loans in high-minority areas is the critical factor in every redlining case. If you go back and read any redlining case, the DOJ frequently cites lending rates in neighborhoods of color as lacking, which is what redlining is—not making loans in minority areas and to minority individuals. While this may seem obvious, regulators use various metrics to gauge lending rate deficiencies.

The first one is like the applications factor I already mentioned. How is a bank stacking up against peer lenders? When a bank's lending rates are two, three, and four times behind peers also making loans in the same area, it is easy to create a case for at least potential redlining. If other mortgage lenders can make loans to minority borrowers and in higher minority areas, lenders in question have less of a defense.

Another factor is the bank's lending rate in white neighborhoods compared to minority neighborhoods. When a lender has no problems making loans in white neighborhoods, but does minimal lending in minority areas, significant redlining risk is present. You may see a trend here—it is hard to argue against simple math.

The third factor, market share, ties closely to the second factor. Regulators look specifically at market share based on borrowers or neighborhoods. When a bank's market share to white borrowers or in white neighborhoods is significantly higher than to minority borrowers or high-minority neighborhoods, high redlining risk is present. Market share can also be compared to peer lenders as an additional metric.

FACTOR FIVE – PRODUCT OFFERINGS

I mentioned several ways that old policies, laws, and prejudice have held minority borrowers back from accessing credit. Decades of redlining and discriminatory policies have created credit issues in some regions. These facts don't mean that minority borrowers are not creditworthy and do not repay loans. Still, their creditworthiness may look less advantageous on paper than white borrowers.

Remember the credit score issue I mentioned earlier? Suppose residents in a community are more likely to rent than own their homes, and those rent payments don't get reported to a credit bureau. In that case, they will have lower credit scores on average. The lower your credit score, the less creditworthy you appear on paper. What does this mean for product offerings?

Banks can tailor products to individuals to ensure they can get a loan. This is their choice of product offerings. Certain loan products are designed for borrowers with less-than-perfect credit.

You may not qualify for traditional banking products if you have a lower score. Some products are in the form of government-guaranteed loans that I mentioned earlier. These products come with a guarantee that helps borrowers get approved. Other products may offer special programs like down payment assistance that reduces payments and lowers an applicant's loan-to-value ratio. A bank that doesn't provide these types of loans in areas where they are most needed will make few loans in that area.

Therefore, banks must know the credit needs of their market area and tailor product offerings to those needs. To truly serve the members of a community, a bank needs to offer attainable products.

FACTOR SIX – COMMUNITY INVOLVEMENT

I am also going to tie this factor to branch placement. When a bank has a branch in any community, they are more likely to be involved in that community. When they don't have a branch in a particular area, the opposite is true, and community involvement is often nonexistent. Community outreach is such an essential factor in banking. It is a highly effective way to get to know the residents in an area and their needs, connect with them, and establish and build relationships.

By that same token, relationships with key community members and groups can be the difference-maker for a bank genuinely trying to serve minority communities. Certain community groups are already connected with community members, and partnerships with these groups can be a simple, quick, and effective gateway to serving an area's population. Suppose a bank has no physical presence in a community. This key factor makes it nearly impossible to engage with the community and its residents.

There can be other factors that drive redlining risk, but these are the most often cited issues in public redlining cases. What happens to banks that go through a redlining case? Well, we have already established that the case is made public. In other words, everyone will find out, which is terrible for a bank's reputation.

Telling the world that a bank is redlining is not the primary objective of the federal government. They aim to solve the problem, and they do that in many ways. However, with the redlining risk factors I have laid out in this chapter, the corrective action required of banks charged with redlining also have common themes. That's what we will talk about in the next chapter.

CHAPTER SIX

HOW BANKS IMPLEMENT CORRECTIVE ACTION

53

Once redlining is proven, banks are subject to formal enforcement actions. In simple terms, the federal government will force them to do certain things to correct the issue and prevent its reoccurrence. These enforcement actions can come from a formal consent or cease-and-desist order. Studying these enforcement actions over time has revealed some common themes. No matter the situation, bank resources, or region of the country, there are consistently used methods to correct redlining issues. Even the DOJ has publicly addressed these common themes. Unsurprisingly, they are tied closely to the problems discussed in the last chapter. Let's talk about these different methods for corrective action now. They should sound familiar at this point.

CORRECTIVE ACTION #1 - OPEN BRANCHES IN PREVIOUSLY REDLINED AREAS.

This one is relatively easy to figure out on your own, so why not figure it out before your bank becomes the next redlining case? Banks cited for redlining issues usually must open at least one new branch in previously redlined areas, sometimes more. Having a physical branch location is an excellent way to embed the bank into the community and meet the needs of its residents.

Opening branches can be expensive, which is one of the reasons why banks don't invest in them even when they know they likely should. A branch bank is more than just office space, although that in and of itself can be expensive. You need a vault, heightened security, potentially a drive-through, ATMs, and office space. Turning a commercial building into a banking location is difficult, so they are often built specifically for banking purposes from the ground up.

Fortunately, there is a cost-effective alternative to moving in the right direction while considering a branch location—loan production offices. A loan production office is different from a branch location because it is only there to bring in loans. There are restrictions on what a bank can do in a loan production office. Still, because it is not a standard bank location and does not accept deposits, it does not need cash on hand. That significantly reduces the security burden. For this reason, you can open a loan production office virtually anywhere, including in currently built office locations, for much less than a bank branch location.

A loan production office will only solve some of the problems of a branch location. Still, it is a quick and cost-effective way to start serving a community's credit needs. Banks that open loan production offices also use them to see if an area will be profitable. If they are successful, it is proof that a branch is worth the investment in that area, and banks often build branches upon those successes.

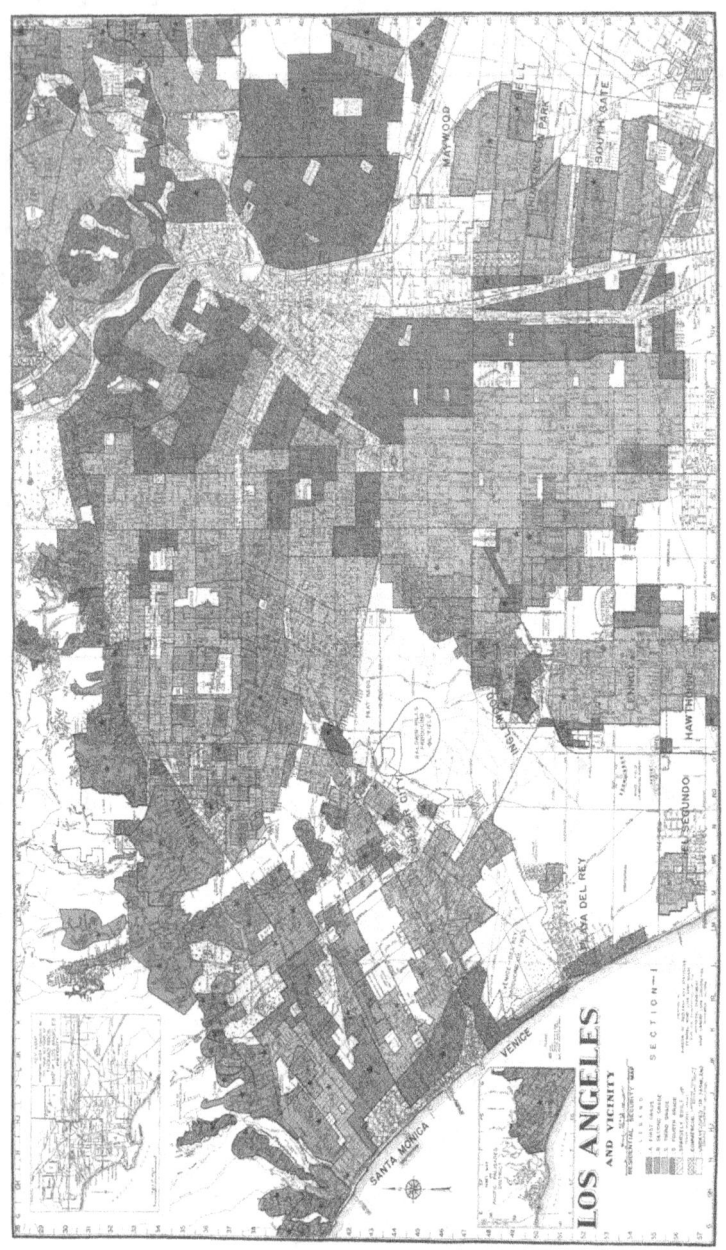

MAP OF LOS ANGELES[5]

CORRECTIVE ACTION #2 – COMMUNITY NEEDS ASSESSMENT

In the last chapter, I mentioned that a bank needs to know the needs of the communities it serves. An excellent way to accomplish that is by doing a community needs assessment. Banks need to gather data on the residents in the community and assess the actual credit needs. Does an area lack affordable housing? Is small business financing a key to community prosperity? Banks need to find out those needs and tailor their products accordingly.

In my bank examiner days, I used to do community contacts as part of Community Reinvestment Act evaluations. I would contact experts in the bank's local area and sit down and ask them questions about the community and its credit needs. If I was examining a bank that was a major small business lender, we would talk with experts in small business lending to determine community needs and if banks were meeting those needs. If the bank I was examining was big into mortgage lending, I might talk with a realtor or government housing official. This was always a great way for me to learn about the credit needs of a community, and bankers should do the same thing.

Banks can also look at their competition and see what products they offer. This analysis is an indicator of what the needs are and how to serve residents in a particular area. A community credit needs assessment can provide valuable insight and a path to success. Seeing the services others provide can point you in the right direction and give you new ideas. Knowing that other lenders are meeting a particular need may also lead you to offer different products or services currently unavailable.

CORRECTIVE ACTION #3 - COMMUNITY PARTNERSHIPS

A few years ago, I asked one of the highest-ranking DOJ representatives a question at a fair lending conference. Since I frequently
perform fair lending audits for clients and teach critical principles
in our fair lending school, I wanted simple advice to pass along to
my clients and students. I asked this representative, "If there was
only one piece of advice, I could give a bank to start addressing a
redlining problem, what would it be?" This person, without hesita-
tion, said to start building relationships with key members within
those communities.

They suggested finding impactful community groups or individuals who understand the community's needs and are working
with residents directly. Many community groups already know
the needs and have connections with community members.
Partnering with them to get involved in those communities can
be one of the quickest and most cost-effective ways to establish
credit relationships in a redlined community. It will also give
insight into which products fit best and will make the biggest
impact.

CORRECTIVE ACTION #4 - LOAN SUBSIDY FUNDS

Almost every redlining case requires some loan subsidy fund
creation to meet the credit needs of an underserved or redlined
community. I have already mentioned why residents in communities of color may look less creditworthy on paper. Our federal
government forced redlining on those communities for decades
and prevented residents from buying homes. Years of being barred
from homeownership and forced to rent without building a credit
history have made those communities poorer. A loan subsidy fund

provides a way to help residents qualify for financing in several different ways.

They can help with down-payment assistance. This fund ensures borrowers can reach homeownership faster by helping them with the required down payments to purchase a home. This lowers the house's overall price, reduces the borrower's loan-to-value ratio, and lowers payments, providing for a lower debt-to-income ratio, and thus making them more creditworthy.

They can also help to buy down the rate. In other words, the funds help pay fees, which can lead to a lower interest rate. A lower interest rate leads to lower monthly payments, ensuring more borrowers can afford to buy a home.

CORRECTIVE ACTION #5 – SPECIAL PURPOSE CREDIT PROGRAMS

Special Purpose Credit Programs are specifically designed to meet the credit needs of areas or residents. These programs allow lenders to build credit products and features to help previously underserved communities. They ensure that small business owners or residents who otherwise would not qualify under a bank's underwriting guidelines can access credit or receive favorable terms. The law allows lenders to offer products to those who wouldn't usually qualify or terms and conditions they wouldn't normally receive.

These credit programs are essential to meeting the credit needs of underserved and redlined communities. The products, services, and terms offered must make sense and be affordable to these communities, or nothing else we have discussed matters. These programs do just that.

Another mistake I see many banks making is similar to other concepts I have already mentioned. It is not wise to look at and copy other banks' Special Purpose Credit Programs in the area. This practice is a bad idea for two reasons. First, the programs others offer may not effectively meet community needs. A bank could offer a better product had they done more research. Second, other products may be needed that could also benefit an area. However, those opportunities are lost if every lender in an area offers the same special credit purpose product.

Like doing market research and a credit needs assessment, these loan assistance programs require the same attention. Special Purpose Credit Programs can be a wonderful thing. Still, they need to be designed specifically for the communities they serve; they're not copy-and-paste types of corrective action methods.

CORRECTIVE ACTION #6 – INVEST IN MARKETING AND ADVERTISING

We have already discussed the lack of marketing in an area as a redlining risk, so unsurprisingly, investing in marketing is often included in fair lending and redlining enforcement actions.

This provision ensures banks that have redlined invest in marketing across the identified communities. Customers need to know the bank exists and what products and services they offer. Marketing is also a way to reach communities needing a physical branch. Yes, it helps to have brick-and-mortar buildings in the community, but leveraging technology is an excellent start to meet the credit needs of an area until a physical branch can be built. It doesn't matter what line of business you are in, selling products is much easier if people know you exist.

Therefore, it's common for the DOJ to require banks to invest hundreds of thousands of dollars into marketing and other outreach efforts in redlined communities. Of course, that is a cost to the bank, but this corrective action method provides immediate returns in new business. Yes, banks hit with redlining cases often pay fines and civil money penalties to the government. That money out the door never gets a return. Marketing dollars do. If you are a bank with heightened redlining risk, it is wise to spend the money on marketing now instead of using it to pay fines later.

CORRECTIVE ACTION #7 – HIRE EXPERTS TO ASSESS THE COMPLIANCE MANAGEMENT SYSTEM

When I heard the DOJ representatives speak on some of these talking points recently, this was one of the last points mentioned, but certainly not the least. Enforcement actions often require a bank to hire a third-party consultant to review a bank's compliance management system and overall compliance program. However, banks need to hire someone who knows what they seek. What does a good program review look like?

I have reviewed hundreds of bank compliance management systems, and many of those reviews were specifically looking at the fair lending program. Here are things every bank can do to strengthen its compliance management system and fair lending program.

Clear and concise policies and procedures are essential. The up-front guidance given to the loan staff must be clear, concise, and free from guesswork. Requiring "no recent late payments" in a policy or procedure does no good. Why? Well, what's recent? One lender will think three months is recent, while others believe six- or twelve-months count as recent late payments. As a lender, do I only care about recent late payments with my bank, or do I care about recent late payments to other banks?

That type of guidance is unclear, so every lender will guess and evaluate late payments differently. That means every applicant will be treated differently, and the risk of that different treatment based on something like race becomes more likely. Every bank needs to read its loan policy and procedures to ensure lenders never have to guess how to make fair and consistent loan decisions.

Training is the next component. All bank personnel should get basic fair lending training. This training should also be job-specific. Most fair lending training I have seen lists the prohibited basis characteristics under the law, the definition of discrimination, and cites a few examples of how other banks have screwed up. That's it, and good luck. That's not helpful.

Instead, training should be job-specific about the different fair lending risks, covering the loan life cycle as I've laid out and each of those risks. This fair lending training should also be part of basic job training. You can hire a twenty-year experienced lender, and they will understand basic loan principles. They know how to underwrite a loan, but do they know how to do it at your bank? Do they know how you calculate underwriting factors, how to get policy exceptions approved, or your loan decision procedures? Do not underestimate basic lender training. Don't assume your lenders know, clearly understand, and follow policy. Spend the time to train them right.

Monitoring and auditing are the third component. Your internal compliance staff should continually monitor your bank for fair lending risks. Periodically, internal audit staff (if you have the expertise in-house) or external auditors or consultants should conduct fair lending reviews. It is nearly impossible to solve problems you do not know about. The larger and more complex a bank is, the more often monitoring and auditing should happen.

Another issue can be how you respond to consumer complaints. Every bank should monitor general complaints and specifically fair lending-related complaints. A general complaint might be someone upset about a fee on a deposit account. A fair lending-related complaint is when someone claims they were treated unfairly in the loan process because of a prohibited basis characteristic.

On more than one occasion, I have seen a single fair lending-related complaint drive an entire fair lending examination. Take all fair lending-related complaints seriously and thoroughly research each one. Larger banks need to monitor complaint trends. Yes, a bank must investigate any single fair lending complaint in any area. Still, five, ten, or dozens in a specific area are likely a major red flag. You need to look for trends to know.

This chapter looked at some common corrective action items frequently included in fair lending and redlining enforcement actions. These can serve as blueprints for any bank looking to expand its lending into communities of color. There is a reason why the DOJ usually includes the same corrective items for all banks hit with redlining enforcement actions—they are proven to work. Let us learn from the mistakes of others and implement these good ideas before it is too late.

We will examine several case studies in the coming chapter, starting with Midwest BankCentre. I like this case study because it is an earlier case of redlining. It is also an example of how effectively these enforcement actions can solve problems. It gives hope to banks facing these problems and communities of color struggling to find financing opportunities. Midwest BankCentre is an example of learning from your mistakes to becoming a leader in the industry. We will then look at a mortgage company and see how culture can play a role in redlining. We will finish the chapter by highlighting the settled redlining cases in 2023.

CHAPTER SEVEN

CASE STUDIES

To illustrate how redlining happens, we will discuss some real-world case studies. I want to begin with Midwest BankCentre (MBC).[6] MBC is an older example, but I like using it for two reasons. First, the issues identified in the MBC case continue to repeat themselves in nearly every redlining case since. I will illustrate the commonalities near the end of this chapter. In addition, any bank hit with a redlining case could have studied MBC, conducted an internal analysis, and potentially prevented redlining at their organization.

The second reason I like MBC as a case study is because they learned from their mistakes, accepted the facts, worked with the federal government (instead of fighting), and used this negative situation to become a leader in their community. Many banks face regulatory scrutiny, sometimes from public enforcement actions, and continue to push back and fight the regulators. MBC worked with the regulators and the community to right the wrongs of its past and help their community prosper. They proved that anyone could learn and change and that there is a light at the end of the regulatory tunnel.

Let's start at the beginning. Since some of the facts of this case are public, we know the data. MBC was a bank operating in St. Louis, Missouri. Like every other major metropolitan area in the United States, St. Louis has a highly segregated population. The geographic makeup of the city has led to many high-minority areas, predominantly made up of Black residents. With high concentrations of minority individuals comes a higher risk of redlining. Remember, redlining is when a lender fails to make loans to minority borrowers or in high-minority areas. Intentional or not, it is illegal.

Under the Community Reinvestment Act, banks select the areas of the community they intend to serve. It's a rather simple process with a few key requirements. The bank's board of directors and executive management staff map out current branch locations and where they will focus their marketing and lending efforts. There are additional rules and requirements to choosing what the law calls an "assessment area," but understand that people decide what that area will be. Banks get to choose their assessment area, within reason and the law's requirements. If their assessment area is not reasonable, regulators will adjust it.

The bank operated and had branches in the Missouri portion of St. Louis. Most of the majority-Black census tracts sit in the northeastern portion of that area. MBC excluded forty-seven of the sixty majority-Black census tracts in choosing its assessment area. In addition, all the bank's branch locations were in majority-white census tracts. These decisions set the table for MBC and how their performance turned out.

Since the bank is a HMDA reporter, the government had easily accessible data at their disposal. That HMDA data was vital in finding the problems. Years prior to the case, MBC paid an outside third-party consultant to analyze the HMDA data. For readers not working in the banking industry, you typically need some type of fair lending software program to analyze HMDA data. While it's not overly complicated data, having good software to review and analyze it is necessary, and software is an added expense. Because of these reasons, many banks choose not to spend money on these types of analyses, which is one main reason they do not uncover their problems.

However, MBC spent the money on an analysis. The team analyzed three years' worth of data from 2004 through 2006. The results showed significant redlining risk and lagging performance in the high-minority areas. In 2004, peer lenders made 6.5 percent of their loans in the high-minority areas, while MBC was 1.7 percent. Rephrasing that using ratios, peers made 3.8 times more loans in high-minority areas than MBC. In 2005, the numbers got worse. Peer lenders outperformed MBC by a ratio of nearly 5.6 more loans originated. In 2006, the numbers improved, but the bank was still behind peer origination rates in high-minority areas by a factor of 1.8 times.

So, MBC had the numbers in front of them. They knew they were way behind in lending in high-minority areas. They spent the resources on doing the analysis, something many lenders fail to do. What did they do with this information? According to the DOJ complaint—nothing. The official complaint filed states, "Until at least late 2009, after being put on notice of the Department of Justice's investigation, Midwest took no affirmative steps to market its mortgage lending services to Black borrowers or in majority-Black census tracts."

I want to pause for a moment and add a little of my commentary on the situation. You may ask yourself why the bank would fail to act on this information. Why would they see such a major risk and do nothing? It is risky for me to speculate on MBC's situation because I honestly don't know. I was not an examiner on this case. However, as someone who has conducted more than

100 fair lending audits over the years, I often find this in similar situations.

Sometimes, management fails to realize the situation's severity. MBC was an earlier redlining case, so there was less precedent on what to do. Today, multiple redlining cases become public every year. Ignorance is the only reason why you wouldn't know how to respond today. At the time of the MBC case, that information was not readily available.

Sometimes, management doesn't know what to do. They lack the knowledge and resources to act appropriately to remedy the situation. It bears repeating that today, there is an entire playbook of how to expand lending efforts, and I've already laid out many tactics. However, I did not invent the playbook. They came from settled cases. If you read the final order against MBC, it lays out everything the bank did to expand lending in majority-Black neighborhoods.

The final point I want to make is that sometimes, key decision-makers either don't get the information or may need help understanding it. Now, you may be wondering how it could have been possible that a bank would spend all that money on a lending analysis and the information never reached the key decision makers (executive management or the board of directors). That's a great question, but the answer can be complicated.

Based on my years of experience, I often see that not every organization funnels information to the top. Not every organization has the knowledge and experience to understand and effectively communicate the severity of the findings. The simple truth is that key decision-makers are often left out of the information loop. Spoiler alert—that fact is not unique to the banking industry. Welcome to corporate America.

Since a bank's executive management team and board of directors allocate resources, they need to be made aware of these problems.

Perhaps they were made aware but needed help understanding the data's severity. I don't know in the case of MBC, and I'm not going to imply, but it happens frequently. Too often, in fact, and it can be a contributing factor to continued redlining and discrimination. Let's get back to the MBC case.

Every bank and credit union in the country is subject to regulatory examinations. You cannot be a chartered financial institution and operate in this country and escape that fact. They are often on a cycle, which means that roughly every twelve to thirty-six months, these financial institutions are being examined by their primary regulators. MBC was a state-chartered bank and a member of the Federal Reserve, so the Federal Reserve was their primary regulator and the regulatory organization in charge of conducting fair lending examinations.

It was through a routine bank examination that the Federal Reserve started uncovering the lending issues at MBC. After the Federal Reserve reviewed the bank's assessment area, marketing efforts, and HMDA data, it was apparent that the bank was not lending to high-minority communities in St. Louis. The examination also discovered that the bank had completed a HMDA data analysis and knew about the lending problems but failed to act.

As with most fair lending and redlining cases, the lending institution's primary regulator identifies issues and refers a case to the DOJ to investigate. The DOJ will bring formal cases and enforcement actions against the lender when a disparity is uncovered that needs to be addressed. Fair lending and redlining cases do not always originate from the banking regulatory agencies. Still, they are one of the key governing bodies that help identify these issues, as they were in the MBC case. As part of the settlement, MBC was required to invest resources back into the communities to serve the needs of the previously redlined high-minority areas.

MAP OF ST. LOUIS[7]

Earlier in this chapter, I mentioned many redlining cases that have been settled since MBC look like carbon copies. Their branches avoid high-minority areas; therefore, they don't receive applications from residents and ultimately do not make loans in those areas. In addition, they don't market, devote resources like loan officers to high-minority areas, and end up as another statistic.

The resulting impact of the cases is that the federal government requires the lender to invest in such resources. In most settled cases, the lender is required to open at least one branch in a majority-minority area, which MBC was required to do. Many cases will also require the lender to market in those areas, which MBC did, expanding marketing efforts across the majority-Black communities. Cases often require educational and outreach programs to the redlining communities, which MBC also conducted.

Another standard settlement agreement is investing in loan subsidy programs to help borrowers of redlined communities get into homes. I have already mention that these programs are designed to ensure residents qualify for financing and often have down-payment assistance programs tied to them. MBC did all of that and more. According to the settlement case, MBC "solicited and received $200,000 through a federal home loan grant program focused on affordable housing. The bank also approved and opened a line of credit to help finance minority-owned businesses and other businesses in high-minority areas to expand their reach when they otherwise may not have qualified."

While MBC's initial reactions to the 2004 through 2006 HMDA data analysis did not meet expectations, their cooperation with the government and willingness to right a significant wrong should not go unnoticed. According to a recent presentation made by the DOJ, MBC not only addressed the redlining issues it faced, but has become a leader in the St. Louis community in lending to communities of color.

The final enforcement in the MBC case required them to open one new branch location in a high-minority area. Since the case, they now have five branches in such areas. More than 400 community members established new banking relationships with the bank within two years of the settlement. These relationships also helped establish multiple new businesses within the previously redlined communities. MBC now banks nearly one-half of the previously unbanked Black neighborhoods in St. Louis.[8]

After reading through this case study, you may be in one of two camps. You may be one of those who look at this case as a happy outcome. Good on MBC for righting a wrong and helping the communities prosper. Or you may say they did the right thing when forced. I am not going to offer my opinion. I look at the facts and realize they should have known the issues and risks but failed to act, but also good on them to go above and beyond to right the wrong.

Personally, I have fifteen years of experience between being a federal regulator and owning an audit company where I see what happens behind the scenes. As a career compliance professional, I see, find, and know the risks. But I also concede that I have much experience in what I do, and compliance professionals do not run banks. Executives run banks, and they frequently have minimal, if any, compliance experience. They only know what they are told, and if problems and risks are not effectively communicated, how can they solve them?

I don't know if that's what happened at MBC, but I know it happens way more than the outsider would ever realize. I also know that many organizations face major regulatory issues and do not act as MBC did. Rather than work with the government to solve problems, they will lawyer up against claims of law and regulatory violations and fight until the end to try and make them disappear. I've also learned that the federal government does not give up. Regardless of how long the fight lasts, they don't just go away and ignore a bank's regulatory problems because the bank's management does not agree with the conclusions.

Heck, these banks can spend millions of dollars hiring law firms to try and make legal issues go away. MBC did not do that. They realized the problem and went well above and beyond to fix it—far beyond what the federal government required. This is why I think MBC makes such a good case study. They were an early case, and they responded the right way. Unfortunately, all the problems they experienced are still happening to other banks today.

I would like to tell you that everyone learned from MBC. All lenders review their HMDA data, know if their branches avoid high-minority areas, and know if they are taking applications from and making loans to high-minority neighborhoods. That would be a nice happy ending to the story. I wouldn't need to write this book if that were the case. Instead, these cases continue to reach the DOJ. Banks, credit unions, and mortgage companies neglect to review and identify risk, and the problem marches on. We need more education in the lending industry, and that's one of the things I'm trying to do. Through education and deliberately anti-racist policies, we can help solve this problem. The federal government has yet to ask me to help write policy, but that does not mean I can't step up and offer the education piece so those who write policy can do something.

In an earlier chapter I mentioned that most discrimination in banking is not deliberate, or at least not overtly in the open, and my experience tells me that is true. What I mean by that is banks don't set out to discriminate. Poor programs lead a bank down that path, not ill intent. However, that is not always the case. The culture of an organization or its employees can be the driving force. I'm also not naive. I might have been born at night, but it certainly wasn't last night. I don't believe all discrimination that happens is not deliberate or caused by bad policies and procedures. For the next case study, I want to give an example where the culture took over and created an environment where discrimination could thrive.

Trident Mortgage Company (Trident) is headquartered in Delaware, and they also had offices in Pennsylvania and New Jersey at the time of the complaint.[9] Trident was the first time a redlining complaint had been brought against a mortgage company. Most redlining cases are against banks, but the Trident case put the entire non-banking mortgage industry on notice.

Trident had many of the classic factors of a redlining case that we have already discussed. The case focused specifically on their lending performance in the Philadelphia, Pennsylvania, metropolitan area. The Consumer Financial Protection Bureau (CFPB) had oversight of the company, and through a review of Trident's performance, presented several facts in the case. The CFPB claimed that Trident was making loans in majority-white neighborhoods while avoiding high-minority sections of the metropolitan area.

From 2015 through 2019, Trident operated fifty-three offices in the geographical area reviewed, fifty-one of which were in majority-white neighborhoods. They had sixty-eight loan officers during this time, sixty-four of which were white. By 2018, they fired two of the four Black loan officers. Other common problems I have mentioned were prevalent. Marketing targeted white individuals in majority-white areas, and as a result, their lending to minority individuals and areas was significantly behind other lenders in the metropolitan area. What stood out about the Trident case from many of the others I've studied was the e-mail communication among employees.

Redlining cases can easily be proven by data, and most are— but this case and the official CFPB complaint were different. You can read the complaint yourself—it's a public document. In the complaint, the CFPB wrote an entire section titled "Racist or

Discriminatory Emails and Photos Exchanged by Trident's Lending Staff." This is what makes this case unique because there was a paper trail of obvious discriminatory comments and behavior among the company's employees. I'm not a fan of racially-charged language, and I debated on including any of this language in my book, but it's important to know what happened. I did not include all of the comments from the formal complaint. If you are bothered and sensitive to racially charged language, I recommend you skip over the next few paragraphs.

The official CFPB complaint (remember, it's a public document) listed several examples of verbatim language they uncovered in employee emails. These are direct quotes from the official government complaint, typos and all. One section referred to several employee comments about properties in minority areas as "ghettos."

> "A Trident mortgage loan officer emailed a Trident online lead coordinator regarding a consumer seeking prequalification, stating: 'This one is in the ghetto. Pass [sic] it along to ian. HAHAHAHAHAHHA kidding.'"

> "A Trident mortgage loan officer sent an email discussing a comparable property that was used in an appraisal, stating: 'This comps [sic] street is like a ghetto and he nows it and if he doesn't that's even worse.'"

One assistant loan officer received a racist e-mail entitled "Being White, reminder" from another employee. That employee forwarded it on to several other employees. Some of the things included in the e-mail were:

- "Proud to be White"

- "You rob us, carjack us, and shoot at us. But, when a white police officer shoots a black gang member or beats up a black drug dealer running from the law and posing a threat to society, you call him a racist."
- "There is nothing improper about this e-mail... But let's see which of you are proud enough to send it on. I sadly don't think many will."
- "BE PROUD TO BE WHITE!"

In full disclosure, there are additional passages of that email with language and racial slurs that I refused to put in my book. The official complaint goes on to discuss additional discriminatory comments to include pictures that are highly racist. The takeaway from the Trident case is that while much of the discrimination we see in the lending industry is because of poor policies, procedures, and practices, overt racism is still alive and thriving, and we must be aware and acknowledge its continued impact on the industry. This is a clear case with all of the normal makings of redlining with overt racism and discrimination piled on top.

While the MBC and Trident cases show similarities within the lending data and performance, they are two drastically different situations. MBC is more of a traditional redlining case, and there are many others just like them. I mentioned that I like using MBC as an example because the issues are repeated over and over again in new cases. Branching structure, applications received, loans originated, marketing efforts, all favor white neighborhoods to the detriment of minority neighborhoods. While the Trident case had many of the same factors, culture also played a major role.

I'd like to finish this chapter with a rapid-fire illustration of rinse and repeat of the MBC scenario with other settled redlining cases. This is just what happened in 2023 alone. As you read through these, look for common themes among them.

City National Bank (CNB)[10] – January 2023
The Facts:

- CNB is the largest bank headquartered in Los Angeles County and one of the fifty largest banks in the US.
- The formal complaint alleged that CNB "engaged in a pattern or practice of lending discrimination by redlining in Los Angeles County."
- This is the largest redlining case in the history of the DOJ (to date).
- Los Angeles County is made up of more than 50 percent majority-minority census tracts, yet only three of CNB's thirty-seven branches (8 percent) were in one of those areas.
- Peer lenders serving the same areas made more than six times as many mortgage loans in the high-minority areas.
- The DOJ settlement was over $31 million.

Park National Bank (PNB)[11] – February 2023
The Facts:

- PNB is headquartered in Newark, Ohio.
- The formal complaint alleged that PNB "engaged in a pattern or practice of redlining in the Columbus metropolitan area." The time period of the complaint was 2015 – 2021.
- During that time, PNB operated thirty-six locations which received home loan applications in the Columbus metropolitan area, zero of which were in a majority-Black or Hispanic area. For reference, 17 percent of the census tracts in the Columbus metropolitan area were majority-Black or Hispanic. As a result, marketing was lacking in the high-minority areas.

- Of the 101 mortgage lenders PNB employed in the area during the relevant time period, 100 of the lenders were white.
- Peer lenders in the metropolitan area took more than seven times more applications from majority-Black and Hispanic areas than PNB.
- As a result of low application rates, peer lenders made loans to majority-Black and Hispanic neighborhoods between 4.5 to 12.5 times more often than PNB.
- The final settlement agreement to resolve lending issues was $9 million.

Essa Bank & Trust (EB&T)[12] – June 2023
The Facts:

- EB&T is headquartered in Stroudsburg, Pennsylvania.
- The formal complaint alleges that EB&T "avoided providing home loans and other mortgage services in majority-Black and Hispanic neighborhoods within the Philadelphia metro area." The time period for the complaint was 2017 through 2021.
- The bank operated four full-service branches in the metropolitan area, two located within miles of the high-minority areas, but they failed to include these areas as part of their assessment area. As a result, over 87 percent of the census tracts chosen as part of the bank's assessment area were majority-white.
- EB&T did not assign any loan officers to serve the majority-Black and Hispanic communities. Management was also aware of the redlining risks as outlined in a third-party report but failed to act or engage in any corrective action.

- During the review period, peer lenders serving the same area generated more than eight times as many home loan applications from majority-Black and Hispanic census tracts. In some years, it was more than fourteen times more applications.
- Low application rates led to low origination rates as peer lenders serving the same lending area originated more than eight times more loans than EB&T.
- The final agreement to resolve the redlining issues was $3 million.

American Bank of Oklahoma (ABOK)[13] – August 2023
The Facts:

- ABOK is headquartered in Collinsville, Oklahoma.
- The formal complaint alleges that ABOK "avoided providing home loans and other mortgage services in majority-Black and Hispanic neighborhoods in the Tulsa, OK metro area." The time period for the complaint was 2017 through 2021.
- In developing its assessment area under the Community Reinvestment Act, the bank excluded all majority-Black and Hispanic census tracts in the northern part of the Tulsa metropolitan area.
- ABOK operated two full-service branches and three loan production offices in Tulsa, all located in majority-white areas. Two of the loan production offices were opened after the FDIC warned of its fair lending risk, yet both loan production offices were opened in majority-white areas.
- Since the bank's physical locations and lenders were concentrated in majority-white areas, all marketing efforts and

resources also focused on those areas, avoiding the high-minority areas within the Tulsa metropolitan area.

- During the review period, peer lenders serving the Tulsa metropolitan area generated applications in majority-Black and Hispanic areas at rates more than five times as ABOK.
- As a result, peer lenders made more than six times more home loans in these areas than ABOK.
- Similar to the Trident Mortgage case, federal regulators found evidence of racist emails shared among bank employees with contents I won't repeat here.
- The final agreement to resolve the redlining issues was $1.15 million.

Washington Trust Company (WTC)[14] – September 2023
The Facts:

- WTC is headquartered in Westerly, Rhode Island. WTC is the oldest community bank in the nation, chartered in 1800.
- The formal complaint alleges that WTC "avoided providing home loans and other mortgage services in majority-Black and Hispanic neighborhoods in the State of Rhode Island." The time period for the complaint was 2016 through 2021, but the complaint also alleges that the bank knew about the redlining risk from internal reports dating back to 2011.
- During the review period, WTC operated as many as twenty-three full-service branch locations throughout its assessment area. All branch locations were located in majority-white neighborhoods, even though roughly 16 percent of the bank's assessment area were majority-minority neighborhoods.

- WTC did not assign a single mortgage officer to conduct outreach, market, advertise, or generate loans from majority-Black and Hispanic neighborhoods.
- During the review period, peer lenders serving the same area generated nearly four times more home loan applications than WTC in majority-Black and Hispanic neighborhoods.
- As a result of low application rates, peer lenders originated more than four times as many loans in those same neighborhoods.
- Bank management knew of these lending deficiencies both from third-party reports and internal reporting from their own compliance department but failed to appropriately act and correct issues.
- The final agreement to resolve the redlining issues was $9 million.

Ameris Bank[15] – October 2023
The Facts:

- Ameris Bank is headquartered in Atlanta, Georgia.
- The formal complaint alleges that "Ameris avoided providing home loans and other mortgage services in majority-Black and Hispanic neighborhoods in the Bank's self-designated assessment area in Jacksonville, Florida." The review period for the complaint was from 2016 through 2021.
- Ameris operated eighteen branch locations within Jacksonville, and no locations were located within a majority-Black or Hispanic area. Roughly 20 percent of the census tracts in Jacksonville are majority-Black or Hispanic.

- The complaint stated that "in July 2018, Ameris' Compliance Department recommended to the Mortgage Division that its mortgage bankers build partnerships with local realtors and community partners to improve lending in high-minority communities and low- and moderate-income communities and that the Mortgage Division conduct mortgage banker training."

- The complaint also stated that "in response to the Compliance Department's recommendations, Ameris created a CRA mortgage banker position. Ameris' Chief Executive Officer offered this specialized CRA mortgage banker job to a person who did not apply for or seek out the role, had no banking experience or relevant background knowledge, and no familiarity with or connections to Black or Hispanic neighborhoods in Jacksonville. During his approximately one year and seven months in the role, the CRA mortgage banker did not originate a single loan. Nor did he perform any outreach or distribute any marketing materials to majority-Black and Hispanic communities."

- As a result of the bank's branching structure and lack of marketing efforts in the majority-minority areas, applications from these areas were well behind peer lenders serving the Jacksonville metropolitan area. Peer lenders generated applications in the high-minority areas more than three times more often than Ameris Bank.

- The application deficiencies led to peer lenders originating more than 3.5 times more loans in the majority-Black and Hispanic neighborhoods.

- The final agreement to resolve the redlining issues was $9 million.

These are highlights of the redlining cases in 2023 alone. It does not take a fair lending expert or statistician to see the similarities among these cases. It really starts with their branching structure. If a bank does not locate branches in minority areas, they are not going to receive many applications from minority applicants. When branches are only in white neighborhoods, marketing will focus on those areas and lenders will focus their lending efforts in those areas. None of this is rocket science, nor should it come as a surprise to anyone.

In chapter five, I covered what most redlining cases have in common. In chapter six, I covered what banks can do to address those issues. Any one of these banks could have fixed their redlining problems by following these simple concepts. It is clear in some of these cases that they maybe did not understand the redlining risk. That's a dangerous comment to make because it implies that you can bury your head in the sand and claim ignorance, and that's not the case anymore. I'm not letting anyone off the hook for the decisions made, and some of the entities included in these cases knew of these risks and did nothing. Either their own internal compliance department blew the whistle, or they hired outside consultants like what my company does to identify these risks and did nothing.

There is no longer any excuse for redlining. Yes, it was made illegal way back in the 1960s, but little was done to prevent its future occurrence or remedy its historical impact. That is changing. Several arms of the federal government, which include the DOJ and the federal banking regulatory agencies, are stepping up to hold these banks accountable.

CHAPTER EIGHT

APPRAISAL BIAS

In the previous chapter, I gave multiple examples of how lacking branches or not marketing in high-minority areas significantly impacts lending in those areas. That's all simple and easy to comprehend. You need to get applications to make loans, and people need to know you exist before they can apply. But what happens when you have branches in high-minority areas, dedicated lenders to serve those customers, and people are applying, but they are getting denied at much higher rates than residents in majority-white neighborhoods?

The most obvious component of redlining is just avoiding high-minority areas. Still, redlining problems can stem from a critical element in the underwriting process—collateral value. Collateral value is how much the piece of property you purchase and use as collateral on the loan is worth. When you buy a car valued at $20,000, there's a good chance your bank will likely not lend you more than $20,000. Sometimes, they will let you go slightly over to finance in fees, but that's about it. In fact, it's better for them to lend you less than the car's value. They like you to have some skin in the game whenever possible. When you put money down on that car, you are more likely to get approved and some-times even get a better interest rate because they take on less risk.

Why does a down payment reduce the risk to the bank? If you fail to make your loan payments, the bank may eventually have to take back or repossess the collateral you pledged on the loan. They will then need to sell off that collateral, and they often take significant losses when they do. This is where the loan-to-value (LTV) ratio is important. Remember, the LTV is one of the legal forms of discrimination.

How does it work? Spoiler alert—just how the name implies. Let's say you owe $20,000 on that car (the loan), and through some source like Kelly Blue Book, the lender determines the car's value to be $20,000 (the value). You will have an LTV of 100 percent. You take the loan amount divided by the collateral's value to get the percentage. In this case, $20,000 / $20,000 is 1, or 100 percent.

If the bank must repossess that car and then sell it for $15,000, they will take a $5,000 loss on that loan. That's not a smart way to do business. While banks only occasionally must repossess collateral, they are certainly not in the business of losing money. People often say that "the bank just wants my car or my house." That could not be further from the truth. They don't want the collateral. They want you to keep your car and pay back your loan. Banks are in the business of lending money, not buying cars or houses. Banks often lose money when they must repossess collateral, especially when the LTV is high. The higher the LTV, the higher the risk of loss to the bank.

How does a down payment change the game and make your loan more desirable? Let's change the numbers a bit. Now, let's say you were to put $5,000 of your own money down on purchasing that car, so you only need to borrow $15,000. That LTV would come down to 75 percent ($15,000 loan / $20,000 value). Banks are more willing to give you a loan at a 75 percent LTV because they are less likely to lose money if they must repossess the car. They often reward you with a lower interest rate because the risk is reduced. If they had to sell that car, they could go down to $15,000 on their sales price and still get their money back. That makes more business sense for them and makes your loan more desirable with less risk.

A customer's LTV is a smart way to help determine a customer's creditworthiness and, as I mentioned, a legal form of discrimination. No legitimate financial institution will lend money at a 150 percent LTV without other extenuating circumstances. It does not make sense. The risk is too high. They want to be sure they will be made whole if a borrower does not repay their loan. Let's say you had a coworker whom you knew pretty well, but maybe you were just "work friends." They ask you to lend them $1,000. To reduce the risk of your loss, they will let you hold on to something worth $500 while you wait to be paid back. Would you take that deal?

We all get the concept. Most of us are going to pass on that deal. How does any of this create a problem for banks and getting loans? The problem stems from how we value that collateral. Are those items your work friend lets you hold on to really worth $500? When we look at the auto lending industry, we see less of a problem. Reputable third-party resources will give fair market value to cars, trucks, and SUVs. Those third-party sources generally don't consider the race, sex, ethnicity, or the neighborhood someone lives in when valuing the automobile.

They might want to know what part of the country an applicant lives in, but not specifically the neighborhood. Automobiles can quickly move and sell somewhere else. However, the housing industry has a different method of determining collateral value—the appraisal process. Unlike cars, houses cannot be easily moved, so how they are valued and where they are located significantly impacts the owner trying to sell them or use them as collateral to borrow money.

If you have ever bought or sold a home, you're likely at least slightly familiar with the appraisal process. A person (appraiser) will analyze a property (a house) to determine its ultimate value. To do this, they use several different metrics, which are all legal and acceptable in the industry. They will look at the age of the home, the square footage, how many bedrooms and bathrooms there are, and if it has been updated or still looks like the 1970s, among many other factors to determine a final value. Depending on where you live, different things can play a big role in the value, such as how many garage spaces there are, whether or not there is a pool, or what school district your home is in.

Appraisers will then look at comparable homes in the area to see what they have sold for. They will try to find houses nearby that are similar in size and characteristics and have recently sold. They will then use those as comparable sales (or comps) as an additional factor to set the value of your home. There are many methodologies for appraising a home, but the ultimate outcome depends on human input and educated opinions.

Appraisers will identify a set of pending home sales and work to narrow them down to the three to five sales that are most comparable to the subject property of the loan. The sales the appraiser identifies determines the value of the home for the loan's purpose. Appraisers use the Uniform Standards of Professional Appraisal Practice (USPAP) to guide their comparable sales selections, and with those sales they develop their value opinions. It's less cut and dry than valuing a car.

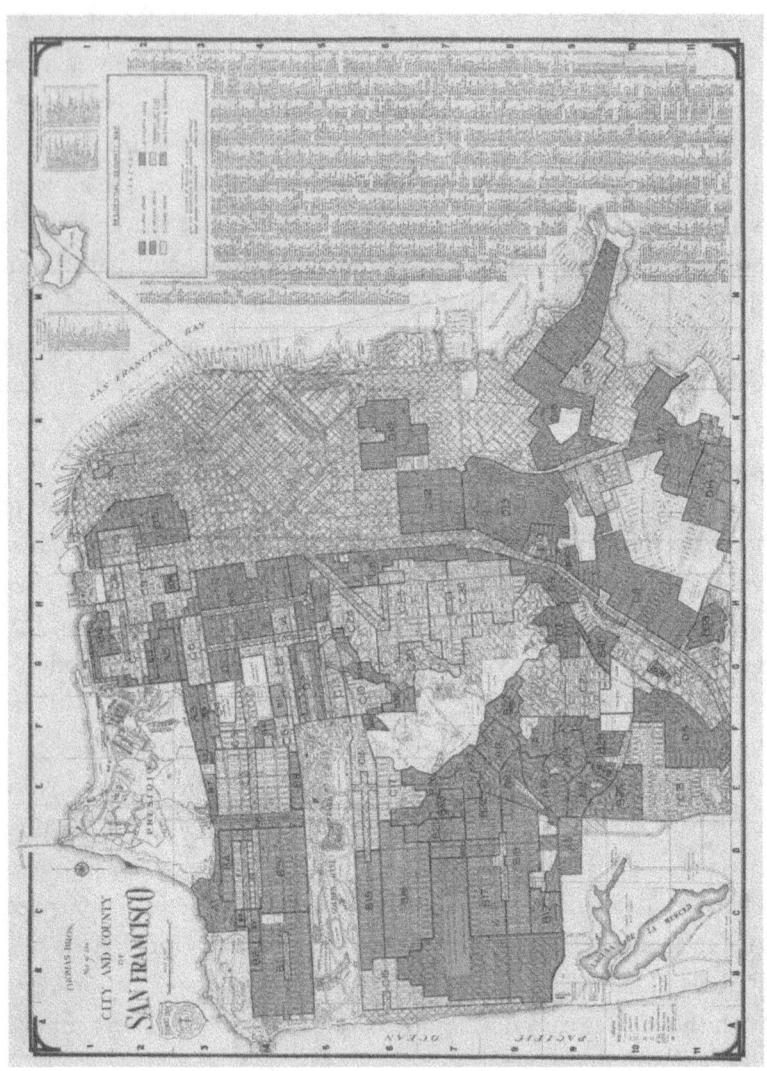

MAP OF SAN FRANCISCO[16]

Becoming a real estate appraiser is a challenging task. Requirements may differ based on where they live. Still, there are often requirements where they must work under a licensed appraiser for a significant number of hours. They must meet other requirements like educational credentials and pass an examination. It's not a profession anyone can step into quickly. It can sometimes take years to become a licensed appraiser, and rightfully so, as those individuals have a critical impact on the residential real estate market of what a home is worth in a financing transaction. Their opinions can make or break a loan, so there is much at stake.

Appraisers have a lot of power and authority to affect a home transaction, but they are also human and have biases. Their job is to give a fair valuation of all properties they appraise. Still, human biases can and often do creep into their work, impacting their final decisions. That means it can greatly impact the applicant's chance of getting a loan.

I've talked a lot about redlined communities. We mentioned how the federal government mapped out every major metropolitan area in the United States. Those areas shaded in red were high-minority areas and were determined to be high risk for lending institutions. While redlining is illegal today, the effects of how those policies shaped our country are still ever-present and impactful.

If an area were "less desirable," the value of the homes in those areas would be less than a similar home in a "desirable" community. To clarify what the federal government meant by desirable and undesirable communities, it was white areas and communities of color. That is not my definition, but the definitions used when redlining maps were created.

That means that a 2,000-square-foot home with three bedrooms and two bathrooms in a majority-white community would be worth more than the same home in a majority-minority community. The difference in values was often quite significant, even if the home in the minority community was superior in quality. Appraisers would undervalue homes in high-minority areas, thus triggering lower values in the entire neighborhood since the sales price of other homes in a neighborhood determines the comps.

Minority borrowers not only get hit once with lower appraised values, but they often get hit a second time with higher tax assessed values. In 2023, Richard Rothstein, along with his daughter Leah Rothstein, wrote *Just Action: How to Challenge Segregation Enacted Under the Color of Law*,[17], a follow-up to *The Color of Law*. *Just Action* focuses on the impact of redlining and offers several solutions to the problem. I highly recommend reading this excellent follow-up book as they outline many ideas that could have a major impact in solving redlining.

I'm a big fan of Richard and his writing on redlining, but his writing differs from mine as he attacks the problem from an overall policy standpoint while I'm attempting to tackle the same problem from the inside of financial institutions. I think both angles are important. Richard is a university professor who studies policy, and I am a federally commissioned bank examiner and now consultant who works with banks to fix these issues internally.

In *Just Action*[18], Richard and Leah point out that minority individuals often pay a significantly higher proportion in property taxes than white borrowers, sometimes double the rates. They point out that "the more segregated a Black neighborhood, the greater are its excess assessments. In the most segregated Black neighborhoods, property assessments are about 60 percent higher than assessments for homes of similar market value in neighborhoods where few residents are Black." This means that minority borrowers are getting penalized twice. The bank and appraisers are setting their home value less than those of white borrowers, but tax assessors are increasing those values, causing them to pay a disproportionately higher percentage of income on property taxes.

With the effects of decades of forced housing segregation from the federal government, it is a pretty good bet that if you lived in a high-minority area, the comps around you were also in a high-minority area. They are your neighbors. During the appraisal process that heavily relies upon those comps, you can see how the problem quickly multiplies and gets out of control.

A home is often the biggest purchase anyone will make, and it's one of the best wealth-building tools. Cars are depreciating assets. That means the value of a vehicle generally goes down over time. Homes are appreciating assets. The value goes up if they are taken care of through general maintenance and upkeep. The asset's value grows over time and can be passed down to the next generation, allowing the asset to gain even more value. Suppose you are a minority homeowner or in a high-minority area. In that case, the value of your home can be greatly devalued from appraisal bias, destroying a significant portion of your wealth, assuming you can buy a home in the first place. That then trickles down through the generations, keeping minorities constantly behind the curve.[19]

Another key wealth building characteristic between buying a home with a mortgage and renting is the effect of long-term financing. The authors of *Just Action*[20] make another vital point. If you buy a home at a set price, you can also lock in your interest rate and payments over say a thirty-year period. That means that for thirty years, your home will increase in value, but your payments will always remain the same. Every dollar paid to the principal will bring you equity in your home and add to your overall wealth—a forced savings account if you will. Renting on the other hand builds no equity. You gain no ownership of the residence. Anyone who has rented for several years also knows that rent also goes up over time. That means a person with a mortgage will have steady house payments for decades while building wealth, whereas a renter builds no equity and faces ever-increasing housing prices.

You don't have to take mine or Richard and Leah's word for it. Statistics of homeownership and wealth for different races are updated on an annual basis. According to recent statistics from the DOJ, the homeownership gap between white and Black Americans is greater now than it was before the passing of the Fair Housing Act. That means the law designed to end housing discrimination has done so little to reverse it that homeownership gaps are worse today than before its enactment.

Overall, wealth gaps also continue to expand. There are many different statistics on the racial wealth gap in America, but they all show the same startling truth. White families have significantly more wealth than Black and Hispanic families. According to a 2019 Federal Reserve Bank of St. Louis study, the average white family had a net worth of $184,000. The average Hispanic family's net worth was $38,000. Black families' average net worth was $23,000.[21] A white family's net worth is over 4.8 times higher than the average Hispanic family and eight times higher than that of the average Black family. This is in large part due to inequality in housing. Appraisal bias significantly contributes to homeownership rates and is one of the major contributing factors to overall wealth inequality.

There are ways to solve appraisal bias. One way is to diversify the appraisal industry. According to a 2021 U.S. Bureau of Labor and Statistics survey, 97 percent of all appraisers are white, and 70 percent are men. There are other statistics that may show different estimates of the appraiser demographics, but again, all show that the industry is overwhelmingly white and male. Some organizations are trying to get more minorities into the appraisal trade, but this takes time. There are concentrated efforts to ensure people of color get the training and have access to the education needed to become appraisers. However, it takes years to become a licensed appraiser, so this will take a deliberate effort to diversify the industry.

What is a person of color supposed to do if they face potential discrimination in the valuation process simply because of their skin color? What many people have done is employ an unofficial concept known as "whitewashing." Whitewashing is not an effective way to solve appraisal bias. Still, it is a way for a minority borrower to minimize its impact on a case-by-case basis. I'll be honest—my ignorance as a middle-aged white male living in the upper Midwest shielded me for years from the concept of whitewashing. Still, if you are a person of color reading this, it's likely old news. Let's catch everyone up on what whitewashing means.

Whitewashing is when a minority homeowner removes every personal effect from their home that would identify them as a person of color. All pictures, anything with their name, or any personal effects that give away their race or ethnicity are removed before the home is appraised. The whole goal is for the appraiser to not know a person of color lives in the home to reduce or hopefully eliminate racial bias in the appraisal process.

I watch home shows on TV, so I already knew taking all personal effects down could help sell your home. Still, I never realized how critical it is for a minority person to do this and how it can significantly impact the appraisal process. When you go to sell your home, sure, it makes sense to take down personal effects. It's hard to imagine living in a home when pictures of the current homeowners are all over the walls. You want people to come into your home and imagine themselves living there. I understand it when you are trying to sell.

But what if you are just refinancing your mortgage? You may be trying to get a lower interest rate or want to take out a home equity loan for home improvements, a vacation, or to start a business.

Why on earth would you need to take down personal effects when you are not trying to sell your home? Appraisal bias and human bias are why. If the appraiser knows a minority family owns the house, and human bias creeps in, that home can be undervalued. That's why so many people of color know they should whitewash their homes before any appraisal.

Don't believe me? The internet is full of stories on how appraisal bias destroys home values for people of color. I do not want to throw a bunch of numbers at you. Google "appraisal bias" if you don't believe me. However, I don't want to leave you with just my word. I like using the power of storytelling to illustrate my point, so let's look at another quick case study.

Paul Austin and Tenisha Tate-Austin are a Black couple living in Marin City, California.[22] They purchased their home in 2016. Their community is close to San Francisco, so as you can imagine, homes are expensive. Over the span of a few years, the Austins did major upgrades to the house, including adding a significant amount of square footage. They eventually wanted to finance the home improvements, so they had an appraisal conducted on their home, which would help them get a loan and access the equity they had built. This is a common practice in the industry that should've been straightforward. In their case, it was not.

Their home was valued at $1,450,000 a year before this appraisal, so they expected to see something around that number or hopefully even higher. We know home values generally go up over time, but short-term shifts in the market can see a temporary decline. However, that is not even close to what happened. This appraisal, conducted by a white female appraiser, came in at $995,000—nearly half a million dollars less than the appraisal the year prior.

Upset and frustrated, the couple filed a complaint to the bank. They stated their case, pointed out all of the home improvements and additional square footage, and claimed that the low-balled appraisal was due to their race. The bank they were working with agreed to order a new appraisal. They were fortunate in this case because often nothing happens when a borrower raises similar concerns, so the loan often dies at this stage in the game.

As a result, a new appraisal was ordered to value their home, and the Austins whitewashed their home before the next appraiser visited. They removed everything in the home that would identify their race, even going so far as to remove hair care products. They were not going to leave anything to chance. When the new appraiser came, they even asked a white friend to be present in the home and put up some of their family photos to make it look like a white family lived there.

I can imagine right now what you're wondering. What was the appraised value this time around? It was still the same house—the same square footage, kitchen, and bathrooms, and in the same neighborhood. The only key difference is that this time, it looked like a white family owned the house instead of a Black family. This time, the value went up. It went up a lot. The new appraised value came in at $1,482,500! This was even higher than the amount a year prior and roughly 50 percent higher than before they whitewashed their home.

If you are skeptical about this topic, I recommend you research. Simply Google "whitewashing," and you will find story after story where this happens. You will discover statistics that show how appraisal bias destroys home values, significantly diminishes wealth, and disproportionately harms minority homeowners.

To end the story—the couple sued the appraiser. There was an undisclosed settlement amount, but what I felt was even more critical was that the appraiser was required to take extensive training in appraisal bias so this would never happen again. Yes, the couple should have earned financial compensation for what happened.

However, the fact that the judge went out of their way to require the appraiser to get fair lending training sends a powerful message to the industry. It shows that financial compensation is not enough and that people in the industry need to be better educated to prevent this from happening in the first place. That's one case and one appraiser. That's a slow way to solve the problem, but it's a start. If banks can learn how to solve redlining issues by observing other redlining cases and the required corrective action, appraisers can learn how to eliminate appraisal bias by reviewing this case.

Unfortunately, there are more cases like this, but how many cases would there be if every appraisal bias instance was pursued? Many homeowners give up and don't hire a lawyer. Others don't know they were discriminated against or might lack the resources to do something about it. Some don't know what to do, so they do nothing. The issue happens often but is rarely fixed.

Appraisal bias is just one key problem in the appraisal industry that has many more flaws. During the research of this book, I had the opportunity to interview an executive and expert in the appraisal industry. This expert asked to remain anonymous for fear of damaging current working relationships with appraisers. For the purposes of this book, I will refer to this appraisal industry expert as Pat.

Pat tells the story of the way appraisals are conducted and how there has been a drastic shift over the years in the way appraisers and mortgage bankers work together. The housing crisis that swept our country from roughly 2007 to 2009 had a drastic impact on the housing industry in general and the appraisal industry specifically. I don't want to go over the housing crisis in detail, as that is a whole book in and of itself, but essentially the appraisal rules were much looser during that period than they are today.

Pat mentioned that appraisers and mortgage bankers had a much closer working relationship. They knew each other well, talked often throughout the appraisal process, and may have had a personnel friendship. Heck, they could be buddies playing golf together, having lunch, and discussing anything they'd like. Pat said there were many highly ethical operators in the industry. Even though there were close relationships between appraisers and mortgage bankers, they could operate together and still ensure a fair appraisal process. Pat said because of these close relationships, mortgage bankers were much more knowledgeable on the appraisal process, and this was a positive.

Of course, the opposite also happened. Lenders could and often would pressure the appraiser to change home values to ensure deals got done. It was common for borrowers to be approved for mortgages that they could not afford but were green lighted because of inflated housing prices. This lead to higher payments that put additional financial stress on thousands of homeowners.

In a separate but related issue, Black and Hispanic borrowers were steered into higher risk products like adjustable-rate mortgages significantly more often than white borrowers. When the lower rate period expired and rates increased, they could not afford the new payments and often defaulted and lost their homes. These were all contributing factors to the housing meltdown, and minority borrowers were disproportionately impacted.

In response to the housing crisis and one of the worst economic recessions since the great depression, laws and regulations were written to prevent these problems from ever happening again. After new appraisal rules were written, a great wall was created between the appraiser and the mortgage lender. Where previously there had been collaboration and sharing of information, everything halted. In fact, someone else at the bank other than the mortgage lender now must order the appraisal to ensure there is no influence whatsoever from the lender. The only thing the lender sees at the end of the process is the appraisal report.

Pat, who frequently works with appraisers and mortgage lenders, says that most lenders now just read the final appraised number and rarely ever read the report. This has led to an industry of lenders who know less about the appraisal process than they used to. They just rely on a number, often never giving value a second thought. If there is obvious appraisal bias, the lender might have no idea.

Pat talks about the shift from having too open of a relationship between the appraiser and mortgage lender to having absolutely no relationship. If a borrower or the lender feels the appraisal is inaccurate, they can challenge it. In the industry, they call this a reconsideration of value (ROV). Pat mentioned that they don't know of any existing rules, laws, or regulations that say the appraiser must even respond to a challenge of their written property valuation. They can simply ignore the request and move on to the next job. This gives appraisers a tremendous amount of power in the industry. They are the gatekeepers of value with no credible challenge to their conclusions.

We have essentially gone from one extreme of unrestricted communication and collaboration to separating key parties where there is almost no discussion, exchange of information, or repercussions. Is there some happy medium where appraisers can remain independent, yet still work with the mortgage lenders to ensure the process is fair, equitable, and open to collaboration? It turns out, there is a program that already has a framework in place to do so.

The Veterans Administration (VA) has a loan program for qualified veterans to buy a home. I already mentioned earlier about how they, along with the Federal Housing Administration, were key contributors that forced redlining and created housing segregation. However, they are now working to ensure a fairer process.

The VA has a long-standing policy in place called the Tidewater process, put in place in 2003. Essentially, the Tidewater process helps ensure a veteran is not overpaying for a home and valuations are generally in line with purchase prices. To do appraisals for VA home loans, appraisers must have a certification through the VA. Through the Tidewater process, the VA appraiser can essentially pause the appraisal process when it is evident through their research that the final appraised value will be less than the contract price. This triggers procedures and communication with the lenders to try and rectify the issue before the appraisal process is completed.

The appraiser will essentially request additional relevant market data to help support the home's sales price. The official VA Circular 26-03-11 directly mentions that "the procedures described in this Circular should in no way suggest that appraisers are being pressured to make appraised values meet or exceed sales prices."[23] The program is designed to promote collaboration and the sharing of key data and facts to essentially prevent appraisal issues and assist in the reconsideration of the value.

Using the VA model, the appraisal process can be more transparent. When it's evident early in the process that there will be discrepancies between the sales price and appraised value, steps are put in place to help remedy the problem. Perhaps the appraiser should be using different comps to value the home. Perhaps there are recent home sales that should influence the value that maybe the appraiser was not aware of. Regardless of the appraised value issues, this process is far from the extremes of the old system where "anything goes" between appraisers and lenders and the current system with no communication or collaboration. Why is this process only used in rare cases of VA loans and not an industry standard practice? How could this help identify and rectify appraisal bias if implemented industry wide?

I do not want to imply that appraisal independence is not vitally important to the appraisal process. The old way of doing things was all around a bad idea. Appraisers must remain independent, and we must continue to ensure that lending staff do not have influence over their work, but there must be a better avenue to challenge conclusions and protect homeowners, especially those most likely to face discrimination.

I asked Pat their thoughts. Pat's main suggestion was to not minimize the need to regulate communications between lenders and appraisers—there are clear paths of abuses between the relationships which negatively impact consumers. However, there were benefits to the communication that the lender and appraiser once shared. The ROV process, made uniform with requirements for training and application, like the VA Tidewater process, may be the place where communication can be retooled.

Pat also shares another unique story. While the borrowers in this case I am about to discuss were not minority borrowers, the problem in this story further illustrates the problem in the appraisal process and how not having avenues for credible challenges can often hurt or kill real estate deals.

Pat tells the story of a home in Los Angeles that was up for sale, and like all cases, went through the appraisal process. The appraisal came back with one glaring issue. The loan was going to be declined because the appraisal noted that the property did not conform to the characteristics of the neighborhood. This issue does happen, but this case was different. The reason cited for not conforming to the characteristics of the neighborhood was because the house had a pool. In Los Angeles, where evidently pools do not exist according to this appraisal (insert obvious sarcasm). Think about that for a moment. Does that even make sense? Well, as it turns out, no.

The lenders challenged the appraiser's conclusions, but for days, nothing happened. No response, and no update to the appraisal. Enter Google Earth of all things to the rescue. Through a simple Google Earth image of the neighborhood, it was easily shown that there were in fact eight homes in the same neighborhood with a pool! Pools are commonplace in Los Angeles, so there was an obvious error in this appraisal that needed to be addressed or this loan was going to be declined.

After several more days of back and forth, the appraiser finally changed the appraisal, and the deal went through. Turns out that a simple box was checked on the appraisal form by mistake, leading to this entire issue. What if the appraiser just chose not to respond to the appraisal challenge inquiry? They are not required to do so. The deal would have fallen through over a silly technical error. Even when the deal went through, it delayed closing by more than a week. This is just another reason why there needs to be more collaboration and transparency in the appraisal process.

There is one last point I learned in my interview with Pat. That is the fact that appraisers can simply turn down jobs in a particular neighborhood they don't want to do. Specifically, if a home appraisal request comes up in a minority neighborhood, they can simply decline the job and cite that they lack "geographic competence" to perform the appraisal.

Geographic competence. That sounds like a fancy term, but what does that mean? As the words imply, appraisers need to be familiar with the market to offer a fair value of properties in the market. You can't simply take an appraiser working in Pittsburgh and just ask them to simply give a value of a home in Houston. That makes sense. They need to have a grasp on the areas they work in and understand the uniqueness of those areas. But the problem Pat describes is that appraisers will claim that they lack geographic competence in areas separated by mere miles or even blocks, where they are more than competent to do the work.

The redlining maps show hard borders of redlined neighborhoods. Oftentimes these are white neighborhoods across the highway, river, or sometimes street from minority neighborhoods. If an appraiser simply does not want to appraise a home in a minority neighborhood, regardless of their reason, they can simply cite that they lack geographic competence, even if they have completed 100 appraisals across the street. Nobody tracks these statistics, and there is no way to prove the legitimacy for their cited reason. People in minority neighborhoods can often wait weeks to get an appraisal completed because of this loophole that goes unchallenged and unmonitored.

Pat also mentions that the appraisal process is standardized, including the need to establish, on every assignment, geographic competence. It is one of the tenets of the Uniform Standards of Professional Appraisal Practice, known as USPAP. However, this process of establishing geographic competence is often being cited to avoid majority-minority neighborhoods, though some will just note they don't cover the area, which they are allowed to do, without justifying the avoidance of the area—another area for reform perhaps.

I don't want you to think it is all doom and gloom. I'm not attacking appraisers, the value of appraisals, or the industry. The point is like lenders, appraisers can have a major impact on redlining, and improvements should be made to the process. I am happy to let you know that from a federal law and regulatory standpoint, things are happening. The federal government is finally doing something about appraisal bias, and rules and regulations are being created to combat some of these issues. Yes, it's decades late, but it is happening. The DOJ understands the problem and has aggressively prosecuted appraisal bias cases. A precedent has been set that now banks and even lenders can be held liable if they rely on an appraisal they know or should have known was unfair. Change is coming. In fact, the federal government is trying to do even more.

A total of thirteen federal government regulatory agencies have come together to form the PAVE taskforce. PAVE stands for Property Appraisal and Valuation Equity. The taskforce's goal is to "close the racial wealth gap by addressing mis-valuations for families and communities of color."[24] Formed in 2021, the taskforce has laid out a three-part action plan:

1. Outlines the historical role of racism in the valuation of residential property;
2. Examines the various forms of bias that can appear in residential property valuation practices; and
3. Describes affirmative steps that federal agencies will take to advance equity in the appraisal process, and outlines further recommendations that government and industry stakeholders can initiate.

Only time will tell if the task force makes a positive and lasting impact on the industry, but at least efforts are underway to try.

Appraisal bias destroys wealth. When a large portion of a person's net worth is in their home, and that home is undervalued by as much as 50 percent, an individual's net worth will go down significantly. It affects people today by destroying their current wealth, and it will affect them in the future when they sell their home. This is a significant contributing factor to the wealth gap in America between white Americans and people of color.

White Americans do not experience appraisal bias like minority homeowners do. They don't need to worry about whitewashing their homes. Imagine an America where nobody had to deal with this problem. What other impacts could this have on minority borrowers? I'm glad you asked.

CHAPTER NINE

REDLINING'S IMPACT ON AMERICA

We have already talked in-depth about how redlining destroys wealth for minority families. Undervaluing a minority person's most valuable asset, their home, will destroy much of their hard-earned wealth. Destroying wealth has widespread and lasting impacts on communities. It continues to drive a wedge in the wealth gap. With increased wealth comes increased opportunities. Access to equity in a home can be a gateway to other financial opportunities.

Accessing the capital needed to start a business or sustain operations until it can be profitable is another critical area where people of color suffer. In 2016, the Ewing Marion Kauffman Foundation researched how people of different races raise capital to start a business.

The article revealed that "entrepreneurs of all racial backgrounds rely on three primary sources of startup capital: 1) personal and family savings (63.9 percent of all employer businesses), 2) business loans from banks (17.9 percent), and 3) personal credit cards (10.3 percent). However, different racial groups rely on these sources in different ways. Asian entrepreneurs rely the most on personal and family savings (73.2 percent of Asian-owned businesses), white entrepreneurs rely the most on business loans from banks (18.7 percent), and Black entrepreneurs rely the most on personal credit cards (17.6 percent)."[25]

Personal credit cards are one of the most expensive ways to access capital. They are unsecured, with interest rates often between 20 to 30 percent. Behind payday lending, this is one of the most expensive ways to borrower money and finance a business.

I want to offer a case study on access to capital and starting a business. This time, I will use myself as an example. After nearly a decade of working in regulatory compliance as a federal bank examiner with the FDIC, then as an auditor, and later a compliance officer for different banks, I decided to take the plunge and start my own consulting business. I had the knowledge, drive, and business acumen to get a profitable consulting business off the ground. I wanted to be an entrepreneur and live the American dream. Besides, I went to business school. How hard could it be? Oh, my young Tory. It's a good thing I didn't know then what I understand now. Turns out it's very hard, but good things don't come easy.

I worked in the background for several months before finally quitting my job as a compliance officer at a bank. I had my business incorporated, built a website, ordered equipment, and made connections. It was "game on" once I left employment with someone else and opened the doors to my new company. I made calls and on-site visits. I sent letters and emails. I offered free training and connected with bankers on LinkedIn. I officially opened my doors in January 2018. After more than five months of grinding, I signed one client for one small job they didn't even want me to complete until the end of the year. Fun fact—I didn't get paid until the job was complete. That was it. After nearly half a year of effort, I had a couple hundred-dollar deposit and one client—cue panic music.

On a personal note, my family had just built our forever home and invested thousands more into finishing the basement. We now had a ton of debt. I'd left a good-paying job for what again? One client after nearly half a year of blood, sweat, and tears? I spent many sleepless nights thinking I had financially ruined my family. The challenge of starting a business is having the grind, grit, and determination to see it through. Oh yeah, there is the money and financing piece, too. Remember, all those bills needed to be paid, even if I wasn't.

I had one major advantage to help me ride out the storm. One major ace up my sleeve, if you will—my home. Our new forever home provided a solution. I like to think of myself as a handyman or a do-it-yourself guy. I hate paying someone to do something I can do myself. I already told you about my curious personality and wanting to learn how things work so I can build or fix them. After spending years in the military as an electronic technician, I was comfortable ripping things apart, using tools, and doing general maintenance and construction. Turns out YouTube is also full of videos to teach you nearly anything you want to know. I have a self-appointed honorary technical degree from the University of YouTube.

I decided to serve as the general contractor and finish the basement project myself. I laid tile and ran electrical, plumbed toilets and bathroom sinks, and framed the fireplace. I painted the walls and ceilings and did just about everything else. When there were tasks which I did not feel I could do a high-quality work, I hired help. I took the names and phone numbers of all the subcontractors who worked on the initial construction of my home and hired back those I needed to help in the basement. I hired others for a few things like sheetrock, trim, and carpet. Still, with some help from my highly skilled friends and many backbreaking hours, I saved tens of thousands of dollars by doing the work myself. I had an asset of value, and now I had equity in that asset. This was my saving grace.

Before starting my business, I asked a few banker friends for advice on how to not financially ruin my family with this crazy business idea. One suggested opening a line of credit on my home before quitting my job. That way, I could borrow against it to help fund my business and stay afloat while building my book of business. So, I did. I got a $100,000 line of credit that I could borrow against with interest-only payments for up to five years. In full disclosure, I would not have let this experiment go on for five years, but I was not prepared to bail after five months either. I knew building up a respected and trusted consulting business would take time. This line of credit ensured I had that time.

I'm a big fan of Dave Ramsey's views on finances. I love his principles on money. He has taught me to hate debt. If you are a banker reading this, I realize that philosophy flies in the face of your entire business model. Sorry about that. While not a lot, I had some money saved that I injected into the business to help with startup costs. When I finally started having revenue come in, I could pay myself back for the money I lent to the business. However, I had a significant cushion of a line of credit. Yes, it took quite some time to start signing clients, but I knew I could always borrow from that line of credit until the business was up and running.

I wanted to avoid going into tens of thousands of dollars in debt before I started making a profit, but I knew it was there if I needed it. My parents were business owners, so I had that entrepreneurial spirit already instilled in me. I knew I could do it if only given the chance. My home ensured I had that chance.

The good news is that I never had to borrow a dollar from that line of credit. Based on my little savings and our other income, I held out and did not need to borrow against my home. I was an officer in the Air National Guard by this time, so I had all my benefits through that career and some additional income. My wife also worked full time, so we made enough to survive. During my sixth month in business, I finally signed my second client. Just ninety minutes after that, I signed my third. Things started looking up. By the end of my first year, I partnered with twelve banks to offer my compliance training and audit services. We have since served over eighty banks, credit unions, and mortgage companies nationwide and counting.

As I write this and put together everything I know and have learned about banking discrimination, I cannot help but think— what if? What if I didn't have that line of credit to borrow from? What if my home was undervalued because of my race? What if I was not afforded the tools and opportunities I felt I rightfully had and earned? I would not have had that equity in my home, and I would not have had that safety net. What if I was denied from ever even buying a home? What if?

I would have used credit cards or likely still be working as an employee. I would be earning roughly the same salary with limited opportunities. While starting a business is tough, the fruit of the rewards make it all worth it. My job running a business is still hard today, but in a much better and different way than being an employee.

I was an employee for most of my life. I was in the military for twenty years between active duty and the National Guard, but I am now retired from military service. I worked for several banks and was a federal employee as well when I worked as an examiner with the FDIC. Being a business owner is entirely different. Yes, you can make more money but also lose it all. Yet, despite the risk, the best thing about owning a business is deciding your future. You get to do the projects you want to do. You get to take risks and help others. But only if you have the opportunity.

Since officially incorporating my business in late 2017, I completed the Graduate School of Banking program. I always wanted to complete that program to become better educated in my industry, but it's expensive. I couldn't convince my prior employers to pay for it so, I paid for it myself. While sitting in a class in that program, I had a life-changing eureka moment. I realized there was no commercially available fair lending school anywhere in our industry. The federal regulators had their fair lending school, but you had to be an examiner to go through it.

Fortunately, I was an examiner earlier in my career, so I got to go through the regulator's fair lending school. Years later, sitting in a Graduate School of Banking class, I wondered why everyone didn't get the same opportunity to learn fair lending as I did. I spent a year creating an educational program to teach others what I had learned. Would any employer, let alone a bank that would see no return on the investment, have paid me to spend a year of my life creating that school? Of course not. I got the opportunity because I owned the business, and I chose what I wanted to do. The school has now successfully graduated more than 200 students nationwide and counting, providing in-depth knowledge of building, monitoring, and maintaining a fair lending program.

After opening the doors of the fair lending school, a wise mentor told me I needed to put my thoughts together in a book. So, I wrote my first book on fair lending in 2022. That gave me more opportunities to teach critical banking regulations to thousands of bankers and compliance professionals. I've spoken all over the country on fair lending and met many great people, and now you are reading my second book. None of this would have been possible without my business, and my business was only possible with the equity in my home. And who knows, I might not have had the equity in my house had I not been born white.

If you happen to be a white American like me, I'm not trying to make you feel guilty for the opportunities you've had. I frequently hear about "white guilt." I'm not saying white Americans need to feel wrong about the opportunities they have been given; just try and make sure others get the same opportunities you have. Suppose you still don't believe that discrimination in banking and redlining takes those opportunities from minorities. In that case, I need to stop writing because I must suck at trying to prove a point.

I'm sharing my story because I want everyone to have the chance to do what I did if they want to. A few years ago, I decided to devote the rest of my working life to ending discrimination in the banking industry. Now that I have a successful business to back me, I can focus on that goal. It's all related. I've been able to help others. I help banks, mortgage companies, and credit unions build robust fair lending programs. That, in turn, helps ensure they give everyone fair and equal access to credit. That leads to others having the opportunity to start their own business, meaning they can help people accomplish their goals. It's an amazing snowball effect.

Think of how many intelligent, driven, and capable individuals never had the chance to do great things. If we continue to expand our reach to more lending institutions, and all those focused individuals who want to start their own business like I did are given the chance, think of how that will spread. They will create jobs in their communities, provide goods and services that may not currently exist, they will pay taxes and give back, and communities will prosper. With additional businesses and homeownership, tax revenue ensures better community services and facilities, lowering crime rates and health problems. Unemployment will decline, and poverty will be reduced. We are holding our nation back by only allowing certain people to succeed. That's what I am trying to change.

I was the youngest of four kids. I already mentioned that my family lost my dad when I was ten years old. He spent months dying of cancer, with no health or life insurance. You can imagine the debt left when he passed. We had hundreds of thousands of dollars in debt in the 1990s, so you can guess how much that would be today. My mom owned her own business cutting hair for a living. Her income wasn't nearly enough to make ends meet, let alone pay off crushing medical debt. We were poor and living off government assistance. For years, we had little, but at least we had food and shelter. I wanted to make something of my life but just needed the opportunity. I started with education.

I got my associate's degree while in the Air Force. I went on to earn a bachelor's degree in communications and a master's degree in business administration. I used the GI Bill to help pay for my education. I then got a great job as a bank examiner to learn the trade. I slowly paid off other debts and started my own business. While growing up poor and disadvantaged, I never had the color of my skin holding me back. Building wealth requires education and opportunity. Imagine how much better our country would be if everyone had those opportunities.

Ending discrimination in the financial world, ensuring everyone has equal access to credit, and stopping redlining will offer so much to our nation. It's not just how we can prosper financially, but physically as well. Redlining impacts the health and welfare of our country—literally.

There are two health concerns I want to address. The first is the socioeconomic stress living in redlining communities puts on residents of color. The American Heart Association used Medicare data to review the risk of heart failure among residents of different geographic areas.

The regions they studied were across the United States, so they included redlined communities. They got summary data from 2014-2019 and race data on over 2.4 million Americans.[26]

The data revealed some staggering truths:

- Black adults living in zip codes with the highest proportion of redlining had an 8 percent higher risk of developing heart failure compared to Black adults living in communities with low levels of redlining.
- In contrast, white adults living in zip codes with the highest proportion of redlining did not have any increased risk of heart failure.
- About half of the excess risk of heart failure among Black adults living in redlined communities was explained by higher levels of socioeconomic distress (determined by Social Deprivation Index scores) in those redlined communities.
- The risk of heart failure was highest in Black adults living in redlined communities that had high scores on the Social Deprivation Index.

As it turns out, simply living in redlined communities has a noticeable impact on heart health for people of color.

Other implications have affected redlining communities for decades. As the federal government would not guarantee loans in majority-minority areas for decades, those communities took in less tax revenue. This had a cascading effect as those communities with less tax revenue had fewer resources, which meant fewer facilities, less money for schools and education, and medical care that did not live up to the standards white communities enjoyed.

On top of that, city planners designed many of the metropolitan areas. As a result, many redlined neighborhoods were in less desirable places, such as industrial areas and near power plants and landfills. The resulting impact on the population was dirtier air and water, longer commutes for employment, and generally poorer living conditions. Living in these conditions for decades affected many residents' health—no wonder those living in redlining communities suffer from a higher risk of heart failure.

You get the picture by now: How much of a negative impact has redlining had on our country? It has destroyed wealth, hindered communities from prospering, created generational poverty, and taken its toll on the residents affected.

I will say it one last time. Lack of education on this significant issue and deliberately racist policies have led us to where we are today. Yes, redlining became illegal more than five decades ago, but we still see it happen repeatedly. I've listed example after example, and many more are in the works as you read this book. Banks, mortgage companies, and credit unions constantly make headlines with unlawful lending practices. Communities still suffer.

If racist policies and a lack of education got us where we are today, anti-racist policies and knowledge of the problem can help solve it. First, we need to educate lending institutions on identifying discrimination in lending. Lending executives need to understand fair lending basics, ensure their policies are free of discrimination risk, and devote resources to high-minority communities.

We must educate the average consumer on why discrimination happens in lending. It's not always deliberate. Consumers need to understand the basics of credit and underwriting so they are better armed with knowledge of the lending process.

The lending industry needs to work harder on creating more loan programs for minority borrowers and low-income areas. It is one thing to weed out discrimination in the loan process, but if minority borrowers already have less wealth, education, and income, they might never qualify for a loan based on the current standards. Financial education, loan subsidy programs, down-payment assistance, and other special credit-purpose programs can all help bridge the wealth gap in America.

Reform needs to happen to the credit scoring model. If the primary way to determine someone's creditworthiness and ultimately if they will get a loan is flawed and discriminatory, we will fight a constant uphill battle until it is changed. More must be done in the appraisal industry to ensure that mortgage lenders and home loan applicants can challenge appraisal bias and ensure transparency in the process.

Finally, we all need to care. I've conceded that it's hard to care about something if it has never affected you. Since I lost my dad to cancer, whenever I have a chance to donate to cancer research, I take advantage of the opportunity. Maybe your family has been dramatically affected by another disease. Some people immigrate to America to avoid war or famine. Others have gone through the adoption process and care deeply about finding forever homes for all children. The point is that we all have things we care deeply about. We have been affected by major outside forces, so other topics that have not impacted us personally tend to take a backseat. That is not necessarily wrong. It just makes us human.

While people of color have much to gain by ending discrimination and redlining in lending, everyone will benefit. Stronger communities, thriving businesses, greater collective wealth, better resources, and reduced poverty are collective benefits. We become stronger when everyone has equal access to credit and capital.

If you'd like to learn more about how discrimination happens in the banking industry, I address that in much greater detail in my first book, *Unfair Lending*. That book teaches the banking industry how to develop programs free of discrimination, but it also offers great insight to the average American on a better understanding of the banking and lending process.

Have conversations, educate yourself and your loved ones on this crisis, and make your voice heard to see real change. When everyone is allowed to succeed, we all succeed.

FINAL THOUGHTS

I brought up many heavy topics in this book. My focus was on discrimination in banking and finance. However, I mentioned discrimination in many other areas and often did not take the time to go into detail on them. That doesn't mean I think things like employment discrimination or police profiling are not vitally important. They are. But my goal is to focus on what I know and where I feel I can make a difference—the banking industry.

My way of writing, teaching, and speaking is to present facts and opinions in straightforward and easy-to-understand language. Complex thoughts and ideas don't require complex language. I simplify the problems as best as I can so everyone can understand, but I am not implying the problems, or their solutions are simple.

Throughout this book, I talked in depth about the problems that weak compliance programs in banking cause and their impact on discrimination. I covered a few concepts of branch structure, marketing focus, lack of lenders, and unclear policies and procedures to make loan decisions. However, this problem of redlining is far broader than just those that make loans.

I am not trying to introduce an entirely new topic at the end of this book. Still, I want you to be aware of the impact other players in the industry have. The problem is broader than just the entity that grants a loan. Another critical player in redlining is real estate agents. Real estate agents have been significant gatekeepers in determining who sees a particular home.

In writing this book, I was told the story of a real estate agent who didn't show an Asian couple a specific home, and the agent said it was because "there is no way an Asian would ever buy a home in that neighborhood."

About a year before writing this book, I remembered that one of the major banks in the United States introduced a special credit-purpose program to help Black and Hispanic borrowers get approved for home loans. A local real estate agent in my community shared the post and blasted this bank. They claimed, "This program is against the law! How can they even do this?" It was blatantly apparent that this agent knew nothing about redlining, discrimination, and how people of color have struggled for years to get home loans.

Their public display of ignorance was quite a sight, but it didn't stop with them alone. Of course, many of their friends on Facebook were also agents with the same company, and they joined in with their public displays of ignorance. It was not only embarrassing to read, but infuriating. How can real estate agents, professionals who sell homes for a living, be so uneducated on this problem? It wasn't until this moment, years after I had been training bankers on discrimination, that I realized there are so many more players in the redlining problem.

Of course, I chimed in. I couldn't be silent. I asked what laws were being broken by this program, only to be countered with "All of them!" I took it upon myself to start educating these real estate agents on the issues, the actual law and what it says, and how not only are these programs not discriminatory, but they are also encouraged. As they often do on Facebook, the conversation got so bad that I finally gave the professional courtesy of telling the author that it's probably best they delete this post. I informed them how discriminatory this looked and how bad it made their company look, and to his credit, he took my advice. The entire post and over fifty comments were deleted within five minutes of my suggestion. All of these agents were white.

As we discussed in great detail, appraisers are also major players in the redlining problem. Pat gave me some great advice. Pat told me about an appraiser group on Facebook that I should join. There was one in particular with thousands of appraisers nationwide that had relaxed rules on joining, so I joined. Pat told me to monitor the page for a few weeks and see the discriminatory discussions held in this public forum. So, I did.

Turns out it did not take weeks to find discrimination. The very first post I saw on this appraiser group discussion page after my membership was approved made my skin crawl. The topic of conversation was the use of the term "master bedroom" and what term the industry is now using instead. I mentioned I'm a sucker for home improvement shows. I noticed over the last two years or so that they don't use that term anymore; instead, they use primary bedroom. Master bedroom, of course, is a term used during slavery, and it is a sentiment to that institution that is still used today.

Some appraisers agreed and said they stopped using that term, instead opting for primary or main bedroom and bathroom. Those comments were met with quick replies and challenges to the change in terminology. One appraiser said, "Nah, just more nonsense. When do we get rid of Master Plumbers, Master Electricians, Masters Degrees?" That comment was challenged with someone saying, "It's called knowing. Don't be insensitive to those whose ancestors were slaves." Several people laughed at that response.

Another appraiser commented on the topic. "They don't care that their ancestors were slaves. They care because they are crybaby people that want to 'change history.'" This person didn't elaborate on what history she implied was being changed. Another person said, "There are currently more people in slavery than when slavery was legal. How are you changing your language for the millions currently not free?" I'm not even going to offer my thoughts on the ignorance of that comment. I've since left the appraiser group. I couldn't stand the amount of hate, open and blatant discrimination, and ignorance. Doing a quick Google search, I learned that in December 2022, there were an estimated 70,000 licensed or certified real estate appraisers in the United States. This is no small problem.

The point I want to end with is that while I do my best to simplify redlining and offer viable solutions, the problem is far from simple. It is extremely complex, with hundreds of thousands of players in the game across many industries. Education is how we make a difference. Education is our best fight against ignorance. Caring, empathy, and being open to change are what will matter. Once we get more people on board, word will spread.

I had a Black friend tell me a story about how he was in a room with hundreds of other people, mostly Black, and they were talking about redlining. The speaker covered the history of redlining and how it was pushed on America from every level of government. Nearly every person in that room of hundreds had no idea of the history. They were well aware of the concept of redlining and how metropolitan areas were segregated, but they didn't fully understand how it happened. So many of those impacted the most don't realize how we got to this point. With that being the case, how is everyone else supposed to know?

Please share the knowledge in this book—that's how. Give it to a friend or colleague. Use it as a discussion topic. I will close with the phrase I have repeated throughout this entire book. Racist policies and a lack of education got us to where we are today. It will take education and anti-racist policies to fix it.

ACKNOWLEDGMENTS

I want to acknowledge and thank all those who have contributed to this book and its efforts to establish equality. While you will remain anonymous due to the nature of the book's subject, you know who you are, and I am extremely grateful for your input. This book would not have been possible without you.

NOTES

1. Richard Rothstein, *The Color of Law: A Forgotten History of How Our Government Segregated America* (New York; Norton Publishing, May 1, 2018).
2. Crossney, Kristen. "Redlining." The Encyclopedia of Greater Philadelphia. April 8, 2024. https://philadelphiaencyclopedia.org/essays/redlining/.
3. Thompson, Cheryl, et al. "Racial covenants, a relic of the past, are still on the books across the country." NPR. November 17, 2021. https://www.npr.org/2021/11/17/1049052531/racial-covenants-housing-discrimination.
4. 5c45f02063ed0.image.jpg (1396×944) (townnews.com)
5. Liu, Jing. "Exploring the Redlining Maps of Los Angeles." May 28, 2024. https://storymaps.arcgis.com/stories/a8f5a063fb664d2da64c576bc6b9cd1f.
6. United States v. Midwest Bank Centre, 4:11-cv-01086 Doc. #: 1 (E.D. MO, 2011).
7. https://images.squarespace-cdn.com/content/v1/5c953be00cf57d0c04964ff8/1565371171358-TRPFHY6QWPFGXGOKRLDM/public.jpeg
8. Department of Justice, Live Conference Presentation, CRA and Fair Lending Colloquium, Austin, Texas, November 12, 2023.

9. Website of the U.S. Department of Justice, Consumer Financial Protection Bureau and United States of America v. Trident Mortgage Company LP, Case 2:22-cv-02936 Doc. #: 1, (USD ED PA, 07/27/22), accessed 03/08/2024, www.justice.gov.

10. Website of the U.S. Department of Justice, United States v. City National Bank, Case 2:23-cv-0-204 Doc. #: 1, (C.D. CAL, 01/12/23), accessed 03/08/2024, www.justice.gov.

11. Website of the U.S. Department of Justice, United States v. Park National Bank, Case 2:23-cv-00822-EAS-CMV Doc.#: 1, (S.D. OH, 02/28/23), accessed 03/08/2024, www.justice.gov.

12. Website of the U.S. Department of Justice, United States v. Essa Bank & Trust, Case 2:23-cv-02065 Doc. #: 1 (E.D. PA, 05/31/23) accessed 03/08/2024, www.justice.gov.

13. Website of the U.S. Department of Justice, United States of America v. (1) American Bank of Oklahoma, Case 4:23-cv-00371-CDL Doc. #: 2 (USDC ND/OK, 08/28/23) accessed 03/08/2024, www.justice.gov.

14. Website of the U.S. Department of Justice, United States of America v. The Washington Trust Company, of Westerly, Case 1:23-cv-00399 Doc.#: 1 (USD RI, 09/27/23), accessed 03/08/2024, www.justice.gov.

15. Website of the U.S. Department of Justice, United States v. Ameris Bank, Case 3:23-cv-01232 Doc.#: 1 (USD MD FLA, Jacksonville Div., 10/19/23) accessed 03/08/2024, www.justice.gov.

16. https://s.hdnux.com/photos/01/03/10/62/17599632/4/rawImage.jpg

17. Rothstein, Leah and Richard Rothstein, *Just Action: How to Challenge Segregation Enacted Under the Color of Law* (New York; Liveright Publishing, 2023) p. 145.
18. Ibid., pgs. 146-147.
19. Website of the Citizens' Housing & Planning Association (CHAPA), "Appraisal Bias's Effects, Challenges and Practical Solutions," Jake Lilien, Counsel for Fair Housing Enforcement, National Community Reinvestment Coalition modified 04/27/23, accessed 03/08/24, https://www.chapa.org/sites/default/files/appraisal-bias-presentation-april-27-2023.pdf.
20. Rothstein and Rothstein, Just Action: How to Challenge Segregation Enacted Under the Color of Law, pgs. 64-65.
21. U.S. Department of the Treasury website, "Racial Differences in Economic Security: The Racial Wealth Gap," modified 09/15/22, accessed 03/08/24, https://home.treasury.gov/news/featured-stories/racial-differences-economic-security-racial-wealth-gap.
22. National Public Radio website, "Black couple settles lawsuit claiming their home appraisal was lowballed due to bias," modified 03/09/23. Accessed 03/08/24, https://www.npr.org/2023/03/09/1162103286/home-appraisal-racial-bias-black-homeowners-lawsuit.
23. Tidewater Process Circular #26-03-11, "New Procedures for Improving Communication with Fee Appraisers and Streamlining Reconsiderations of Value," the Veterans Benefits Administration, Department of Veterans Affairs, December 22, 2003.

24. Prompt Appraisal and Valuation Equity (PAVE)/Housing and Urban Development website, "Closing the Racial Wealth Gap by Addressing Mis-valuations for Families and Communities of Color," Action Plan to Advance Property Appraisal and Valuation Equity, modified 03/22, accessed 03/08/24, pave.hud.gov/sites/pave.hud.gov/files/documents/PAVEActionPlan.pdf.

25. Website of the Ewing Marion Kauffman Foundation, "Startup Financing Trends by Race: How Access to Capital Impacts Profitability," modified 10/24/16, accessed 03/08/24, https://www.kauffman.org/entrepreneurship/reports/startup-financing-trends-by-race-how-access-to-capital-impacts-profitability/.

26. American Heart Association website, "Redlining linked to higher heart failure risk among Black adults in U.S.," modified 07/17/23, accessed 03/08/24 https://newsroom.heart.org/news/redlining-linked-to-higher-heart-failure-risk-among-black-adults-in-u-s.

ABOUT THE AUTHOR

Tory Haggerty is the President and CEO of Tuscan Club Consulting, a professional firm specializing in consumer compliance regulatory reviews and fair lending audits. He is also the President of Tuscan Club University. The university offers the nation's premier fair lending school, designed to teach industry professionals fair lending principles on building, maintaining, and auditing compliance programs to eliminate discrimination in the industry. He also created the Fair Lending Expert (FLE) certification program, an industry-respected certification showcasing the certificate holder's knowledge and skills in fair lending.

Tory's passion to educate and make a difference in ending discrimination is the focus of his banking career. He has dedicated his efforts to educating the industry on the practices that lead to discrimination and how every banker can make an impact. He is also the author of *Unfair Lending: Why Discrimination in Banking Still Exists and How to Prevent It*. Several thousand copies of his first book have been distributed, and it earned the best-seller designation on Amazon.

Outside of the banking industry, Tory enjoys many sporting activities. He is a seven-time state dart champion, an average bowler, and a terrible golfer. He enjoys traveling with his wife and kids and is a major baseball history buff. Tory has been to all thirty Major League Baseball stadiums and loves reading books on the game's history. In 2020, Tory retired as a South Dakota Air National Guard officer with over twenty years of distinguished military service. Tory is also a lifelong musician. He plays guitar, drums, banjo, ukelele, and many other instruments.

www.ingramcontent.com/pod-product-compliance
Lightning Source LLC
Chambersburg PA
CBHW071504220526
45472CB00003B/913